THE AUM OF ALL THINGS

THE

AUM OF ALL THINGS

Ruzbeh N. Bharucha

Author of *The Fakir* Trilogy and *The Last Marathon*

FULL CIRCLE

THE AUM OF ALL THINGS

First FULL CIRCLE Paperback Edition, 2013
First Reprint, 2013

ISBN 978-81-7621-247-2

Editor: Kamakshi V.F., Humata Gandhi, Sudhir Chada
Cover Design: Karina & Sudhir Chada
Author's Photograph: Shantanu Sheorey

Published by arrangement with the author

Published by **FULL CIRCLE** *PUBLISHING*
J-40, Jorbagh Lane, New Delhi-110003
Tel: +011-24620063, 24621011 • Fax: 24645795
E-mail: contact@fullcirclebooks.in • *website:* www.fullcirclebooks.in

Designing & Typesetting: *SCANSET*

J-40, Jorbagh Lane, New Delhi-110003

Printed at Manipal Technologies Ltd., Unit -5, Manipal - 576 104, Karnataka

PRINTED IN INDIA

13/13/05/02/100/SCANSET/MTL/MTL/MTL/OP250/NSP250

To

Sai Baba of Shirdi

The Universal Mother

The Lord Almighty

All Perfect Masters

The Oneness Family

Archangels & Angels

Guides & Light Workers

THE AUM OF ALL THINGS

This book took me out of my comfort zone for the simple reason I am not much into intellectualising God or spirituality. My favourite quote is from the *Autobiography of a Yogi*, by *Paramhansa Yogananda*, where it is stated that "God is simple, everything else is complex".

For me, God is filled with love and compassion and when one needs a whack, our Old Man very grudgingly obliges. He isn't an authoritarian, neurotic dictator or a dogmatic school teacher, but more like an indulgent Grand Parent, who is filled with fun, frolic, compassion and can also be a disciplinarian if the need be. God is cool and kind and has a wicked sense of humour and a faith – bordering on the ridiculous – in mankind's ability to spread His Light.

Thus, the fastest way to knock me off to sleep is to rationalize or intellectualize spirituality or the workings of God.

Unlike *The Fakir* trilogy, which speaks simply about love, faith and surrender to your Master, this book mainly focuses on using your mind and gaining knowledge to move towards Him. My very close loved ones, who truly know me, are aware that when knowledge was being handed out in Heaven, I was standing in the queue where faith and astral cigarettes were being dished out liberally.

Thus, I am a firm believer in the philosophy of Oneness and Faith. For me all spiritual ideologies might take you to the doors of heaven but it is only selfless love, compassion for all and complete positive surrender in the Master that will enable one to enter and walk through that ever open but rather elusive door of heaven.

Death is one of the most inappropriate words to describe an individual passing over to the other side. Death means to cease to exist or the end of life. If you believe that one simply ceases to exist after leaving the body, then its best you shut this book now and give it to somebody, who, like me is insane enough to believe that life continues even after one leaves the body.

Often in my prayers and during channelling sessions, it has been revealed that there are countless ways to meditate and innumerable paths to reach one's God and Master. Some go about trying to find God or themselves, serving one and all selflessly. Others reach God through Oneness and love; some by being pure, noble, honest-to-God good human beings. Many go about seeking God through compassion while some through joyous faith. Yogis and sages are certain that through meditation and or by tying themselves in yogic knots and working on their *Kundalini*, Big Daddy up there is going to grin and be pleased as punch. Several people also use intellectual visualization to pray or meditate using their *Jñān* or knowledge and their intellect through scholarly pursuit. Thus, there are countless paths and The Creator and Master is All Merciful.

Are we created in the image of the Creator? Well that is truly simple to answer. Do you believe you are the spirit in the body or you are the body? If you believe you are the body, then good news! Shut the book and go about your life. If you believe that you are the spirit in the body, that you are the energy that exists and that the body is the container to your spirit, then you are stuck with me.

My logic or illogic is simple. If I am the spirit within this truly battered body of mine, then I have to come out off and from the One who is the Original Spirit. I mean one couldn't have come out of thin air. If we come out off and from the Original Spirit, then we are the embodiment of all that which the Original Spirit inherently personifies within itself. If God is an eternal Flame, then we are sparks from that Flame. Thus, whatever the Flame epitomizes, the spark embodies too.

From the seed of an apple, oranges don't spring forth. The seed of an apple brings forth the apple tree and then the fruit too. Similarly, we who are the spark are the fruit of the Gorgeous Tree which has come from That One Eternal Seed. Whether God likes it or not, each of us has Godhood in a dormant state, waiting to blossom within, once the true reality of the state of "I am That" or *Aum Tat Sat* is realized. Yes, all seeds don't grow into trees but every seed has the potential and capability, to become a fruit laden tree, with the right kind of nurturing.

Unfortunately, nowadays people are insistent that if one doesn't follow *only* their Master or Faith or Philosophy, one is doomed for eternity, to burn in the bowels of hell, where a large man not too clued about appropriate dress sense or personal hygiene and with a truly bad after-shave, thrusts hot rods in various openings in one's astral anatomy. But in reality all Perfect Masters and Prophets are adamant and clear that God is One and that He is All Merciful and there are different ways to reach Him and tickle the Old Man's funny bone.

This is a book about Oneness. This is a book about returning to one's roots. Go beyond the obvious and you will understand that the only thing that really matters is to realize the Oneness of it all. That's why the title, *The Aum Of All Things*.

The word *Aum* doesn't belong to any religion. *Aum* is the sigh of the cosmos. Where the silence is most profound, one hears *Aum*. It goes beyond religion. The Bible says first there was The Word. That primordial word I believe to be is "*Aum*" or "*Ahun*".

This book is about at least acknowledging that we in reality are from the same source and thus we are one. Yes we go about life, like a herd of horny bulls, in a very poorly stacked china shop. We do know very well that what truly matters is all within us, but we still go about making a mess of our potential, capabilities, time, and energy, running after things, or indulging in things, that slowly but surely cuts our own feet; but we don't care or stop. We keep piling up the karmic account and then when things aren't working the way we want them to shape up, we look heaven bound and blame God to be heartless or deaf. The poor Chap isn't even involved in the scheme of things. It's like a man who kills ten innocent people, and then when he is imprisoned and to be hung, he turns around and blames his parents for not helping him to be released. What can the parents do? The Court has passed its judgement. They can appeal but if that is shot down, they have nowhere else to go. How are they even involved in the larger scheme of law and order of the country? Even those who are the founding fathers of law and order in a country, have to then abide with what they themselves have laid down as foundations of law and order in the country. The one who writes the Constitution of the country is then bound to all that which the Constitution contains. So is God. The laws of Karma spare nobody. Not even Gods who have come in human form. So let us leave God out of our misery.

What is Karma? Free Will used at some point of our existence, whether in this life time or the past ones, become in the present and future our Karma; our destiny. Which means it's all about using one's Free Will. So when we started out, we had only Free Will. The pot of existence contained only Free Will. Then through Free Will we formed Karmas and as we used our Free Will, our Karmas shaped our lives and then slowly the percentage of Karma began to rise and then filled the jar of existence. So our present Karma is our past Free Will; if used wrong we experience the ramifications and if used right we gain from the right use of our Free Will. God isn't involved in our Free Will or Karma. That is our responsibility. This is my limited understanding of Karma.

Yes, the only One involved and who can do something in this mangled business of Karma, is the King; one's Master. But then leave it to Him as He knows best. Prayers can either segregate the load into small bundles that can be lifted without breaking one's back or make you strong enough to go ahead and lift the karmic baggage or cross.

None of us, however aware we are – that in reality, only being calm, centred, giving and noble, is the right way to go about this life and the beyond – we still go about making a hash of it all. We all know we are going to leave this body and not be able to take anything with us, but our karmic balance sheet and the love of our Masters and of those who we have shared love and joy with....Yet we hunger for all the crap in the world and go about like demented dogs chasing cars; no real sense and no real purpose.

We all are human and thus we all have weaknesses, limitations, dark corners lurking within us. Self destruction is embedded into our DNA. Be it destroying our Mother – our planet who so lovingly shelters us and loves us in spite of and despite us always disregarding and constantly violating her – or by complicating our own karmic journey, we go about blindfolded, stepping on the accelerator, driving down the wrong way on a one-way street.

I believe each one of us has innate goodness and Godhood in varying degrees of dormancy. But no matter how depraved an individual is, each person will have some redeeming quality that one can observe and learn from. Sometimes one can realize not only from the individual's strength and goodness but learn more from his or her weaknesses too. Lord *Datta Guru* or Lord *Dattatreya*, the first primordial Guru, had twenty-four Masters from whom He had learnt specific truths of life. These Gurus included a snake, a dove, a butterfly, an elephant, an eagle, a bee, a child, a girl, an arrow-maker, a deer, a python, a spider, a wasp, a fish, apart from the earth, the air, the space, the water, the fire, the moon, the sun, the ocean and a prostitute. This is because Lord *Datta Guru* learnt something positive or soul-enhancing through each of the above mentioned beings and elements of nature. So I hope from this book either one learns a few truths about how knowledge can help us get closer to The Creator or how one needs only love and surrender to merge with one's Master and Lord.

If nothing else, if this book can bring you closer to your real self, your higher self, it will make this above never ending monologue worth the effort.

2

I met *Bapuji* and *Mataji*, one cold day in Delhi. They lived in a newly made *Āśrăm* that was built some distance from *Gurgaon*, which by itself is a very thriving city, with an obsession with malls; like huge gigantic pimples on a Giant's arse. *Viraf Mohta*, my cousin, accompanied me.

We seven cousins had all lived in one house in Mumbai, along with our maternal grand-mother. *Viraf* and I had studied at *Billimoria High School*, in *Panchgani*. He was visiting from the US, we both were in Delhi around the same time and he decided to come along. We both went to the *Āśrăm*, along with *Shyam Tandon*. *Shyam's* mother with respect is referred to as *Mataji* and her grand-daughter *Sakshi*, is married to *Bapuji's* son, *Anant*. Thus, it's a close-knit family of spirituality too.

A half hour drive later we reached this small *Āśrăm* – very well kept, with adjacent fields that gave it a quaint look. I can only imagine that in a few years from now, all the fields will be transformed into concrete residential blocks interspersed with shopping malls. We are a nation obsessed with malls.

Mataji was eagerly waiting for me. I had never spoken to her before but she embraced me warmly and spoke of my homecoming. For a long time she inquired about my wellbeing as a mother would of her child; a truly very humbling experience. There is a meditation hall where *Viraf* and I were taken.

"*Bapuji* usually never leaves his room now but he will

meet you. He can give you answers to each-and-every question about anything and there is no doubt about it. He knows all about science, astrology, the *Vedas,* the Holy Hindu scriptures, history, geography, so you can ask him any questions you would want to." Throughout the interviews and research of this book, whenever *Mataji* spoke of *Bapuji* there was genuine love and respect; one witnessed surrender and selfless love in all its true meaning when she spoke of *Bapuji*.

I asked *Mataji* about her spiritual journey. She was a married woman who had children and now she lived in an *Āśrăm*. That couldn't have been easy. Being spiritual and seeking spirituality is one thing. Swimming against the tide of norms set by society, particularly being a woman in India, is a different ball game all together.

"From the very beginning, I had many questions running through my mind. I was about twenty-five years old and had children. I wondered about creation and existence of the world. The moon, the stars, the sun, the earth; aren't these all miracles that God has created?"

I nodded. This is so true and yes, we take the sky, the stars, the planets, the galaxies, our Mother Earth all for granted; the air we breathe, the water that quenches our thirst, Mother Earth that keeps selflessly giving and giving, while we keep plundering Her! Intellectuals I know keep harping about the Big Bang Theory. That all of creation as we know it, came from a Big Bang. That everything was created by this mysterious Big Bang.

If you look at nature around you, our own very complex anatomy, meticulous workings of nature, and I am supposed to believe all this was created by a *bang*? And what came before the Big Bang? The word "bang" means to "hit-beat-whack-hammer-bash-smash". So for any sort of a *bang*, logically there have to be at least two things that need to bang themselves about; two things at least to collide or whack about to bring about the Big Bang and all I want to know, Lord love a defrosted duck, who created the stuff that created those things that created the Big Bang. I focused on *Mataji* once again.

"So I kept searching for answers. When was all this created? Why was all this created? After death where do we go? Where are we born again? How does all this work? What are the accounts and calculations of Karma or actions that lead to one's destiny? On what philosophy is Karma based? I would ponder upon these queries in my heart. I read the *Gītā*. (The *Gītā* is the Hindu Holy text that is a part of the Māhābhāṛăta.) I have not read it many times, only once or twice. Initially, when *Bapuji* would give me *Jñān* or knowledge, I would not understand it. It also included knowledge about astrology, that there are so many *Năkśătṛăs* or planetary configurations in the zodiac, so many *Rāśis* or zodiac signs, so many planets, I would not understand much.

"We have often been told that the world will be destroyed. I do not like the word 'destruction'. It was only when *Bapuji* gave me more knowledge, then I got this thought in my mind that 'change', 'revolution', or 'transformation' is in a way destruction of the old and the beginning of the new.

"And, this explanation about change and revolution and transformation I understood with greater clarity. The whole of *Sṛuśti* or nature is going through a change; a transformation at the subtle, intangible or ethereal level.

"We cannot see the wind. But, we can feel it. So it is with the soul. We cannot see the soul but that doesn't mean the soul doesn't exist. But I began to wonder what kind of a thing is the soul? How are Karmas formed? Why do Karmas come into our destiny? How do they come about? *Bapuji* gave me the answers to all these questions. *Bapuji* taught me. But when *Bapuji* teaches, the understanding comes directly to the soul. *Bapuji* imparts knowledge to thousands of people. But in those thousands there may be just one who might truly understand all what he teaches. Ever since *Bapuji* was a child he used to think a lot about *Viśwa Parivàṛtăn* which means transforming the world. He too would complain to God: 'See, people don't get to eat, they are so sad. What are you doing sitting up there?'

"There are so many energies up there, so many, that through just an *Anś Mātṛ* that is one miniscule speck, there are innumerable *Anant Koti* or innumerable crores of *Brāhṁāñḍs* or creations that are created and exist. All this knowledge we have gained from *Bapuji*. He says that 'The One Above gives me Knowledge'. When he goes into *Yog* or a meditative state that is when the knowledge emerges in him. So when *Bapuji* gives knowledge, not everyone is capable of understanding it. But now I think it is time that the knowledge of 'Oneness' is spread. Initially, there will be just five or seven souls who will take lead. Understand everything first, then we shall see how to move forward. Gain the knowledge that, in the beginning was the Creator and through the Creator came the primary 108 souls. Thus, these 108 souls are the Seed Souls. In each religion, we are taught to pray on a 108-seeded rosary or prayer beads, so what we are actually doing is, acknowledging these 108 Seed Souls. Then through the 108 Seed Souls came about 16,000 souls. Then from 16,000 come about nine lakh (nine hundred thousand). This is how it kept on increasing. So, these initial few Seed Souls, we must catch hold of, impart them with knowledge, that they have forgotten due to *Māyā* or the illusion of identifying with the body and the five senses, get them to perform *Yog* and bring about transformation in the world. These souls have so much power within them that they can bring about great transformation in the world."

"So how does one get those 108 Seed Souls together?" I inquired.

"You will do it, right?"

I nearly fell off the chair.

"You have arrived here and it is the right time now. The time too should be right. Just like how I performed *Yog* and made this place. This *Āśrăm* was made in ten months. In India it takes more than a year to even make a small flat. This *Āśrăm* with so many rooms and buildings has taken shape in less than a year! Can anyone make this place in ten months? In a time span of eight to ten months, in a country like India, at such a remote location? No one can construct such a place, as swiftly! The One Up there is making us do it. It is all the inspiration from up above. So here you are to write the book. What made you agree to write a book on a philosophy that doesn't really appeal to you and even though you are so busy with writing and channelling. Somebody must have created circumstances that you agreed to write this book."

This I could not deny. I had declined a number of offers to write books on varied subjects. I was busy with channelling and getting on with my new book. *The Fakir* trilogy was doing exceedingly well. *The Last Marathon* had been reprinted on readers' demand. There were daily mails and requests for another fiction book. The reason I agreed to write this book was that a year prior to my meeting *Bapuji*, I was taught a meditation technique. It came through while saying my prayers. It had worked rather well for me and for the few people who I felt were serious seekers. Then *Shyam Tandon*, who is *Mataji's* son, spoke to me about *Bapuji* and in general mentioned about a particular meditation technique which was virtually the same as the one I was taught by *Bābā Sai of Shirdi.*

Also, I truly believe that we all came from the One Great Spirit, either directly or we came through the primary

Spirits that emerged from the Great Spirit; which was very similar to the philosophy of the 108 seed souls *Bapuji* had divulged to *Mataji* and to his other followers.

"So before anything, comes a *Sañkalp,* which means a promise (an oath, a vow, a thought, a word, a decision, a dedicated pledge and a determination). So, depending upon our *Sañkalps,* the atmosphere around us keeps on changing. Only our *Sañkalps* revolve around us all the time. Our *Sañkalps* are the atmosphere or ambience or environment that gets created by us and around us. That same atmosphere influences us within and even those who enter into our atmosphere get affected by our intention and vow."

"When did this journey of yours begin, from childhood or later on?" I inquired.

"When the heart aches, that is when the search begins. If the heart is pleased and satisfied, why will one venture out or set out on a search? When the heart is sad that's when it seeks."

How did you go about it?"

"By asking earnestly the first question, 'Oh God, do You exist or not? Oh God, if You are there then where are You?' I would keep on thinking the same thing and repeating the same to myself. Then step-by-step and secretly I started to visit the *Brahmakumari* centre.

"This was after my marriage. At home, we lived in a family with many members, and no one would allow me to go out. They had heard that if you went to the *Brahmakumaris* then you might be influenced to leave your home and family, which is not true. Eventually, I would leave my home and family to live in an *Āśrăm,* but I did not leave my home then. Also, I was of the firm belief that if God exists then He has to be *Nirākār* or formless. God does not exist in idols. Whenever, I would perform the *Ārti* which involves lighting oil lamps as a prayer ritual,

I would think that I am committing a fraud or putting up an act. That praying to an idol is an absolute lie or a farce that is being performed. I would end up feeling that the essential truth was missing in the whole ritual of me performing the *Ārti*. You see, one does not always know how much *Śakti* or energy, one has. Like you for instance, do not know who you are. But I know. I know that it is going to be you only, through whom this work is going to be done."

Oh how I wish my family and friends were with me to hear all this. But then on afterthought I realized it was better that the family and friends were not present. They would have rolled on the floor in an obscene display of laughter.

"So, what happened after that?" I inquired, as the mental image of my dear ones laughing their guts out wasn't something one likes to indulge in.

"Since I had started to visit the *Brahmakumaris,* conflicts had increased at home. Eventually at the age of fifty I left home and began to live in *Bapuji's Āśrăm* in *Ahmedabad*. I am sixty-seven now. Of course, on and off, I had left home earlier too. I would leave home and disappear in my search, maybe for a fortnight or more, then return. I would come back and again find that my heart was not at ease at home. This kept on happening. Then at *Brahmakumaris* the *Sañkalp* or vow took place. That's when I thought that God must also be there in the *Sākār* form or a physical, gross form somewhere at least! For in our religion, we also believe that God is in the *Sākār* or gross and physical form of reality. So there must be a God in physical form somewhere, here, there, or anywhere.

"I kept searching for God. Went to many places and sat in many lectures and learnt many philosophies. My children were with me, they supported me from within and they stood by me. They were sure what I was doing was right. But to leave little kids is not easy. I know you understand very well what it is to lose one's children. So, I kept on fighting and struggling for the truth and the conflict of living or not living with the family.

"There's a saying that suggests a spiritual state of being: *'destroyed all attachments to discover spiritual progress; divine knowledge thy sole quest'* and it became my state too. *Vairāgya,* which means disenchantment from worldly matters, entered my life. In the growth chart of spiritual progression, post *Bhakti* which means devotion, comes *Jñān* that is knowledge. Knowledge brings disinterest in worldly matters. When you understand reality, you get *Vairāgya* and lose interest in all worldly matters. So in my search to discover, I reached *Bapuji.* And he answered all my questions and settled my doubts.

"So, what is my aim now? The existing world is made up of the five elements – *Dhàṛti, Jal, Agni, Vāyu,* and *Ākāś;* that are Earth, Water, Fire, Wind and Ether. These elements need to be changed with *Yog-Śakti* that is through the power of the meditative state. But how will the transformation come about? The air, environment, atmosphere, ambiance is all so polluted! How will it change? With *Yog-Śakti* it can change. New and varied inventions will come into being. Cars will work on water and sunlight, while other fuels will be invented where petrol will not be needed. By the way, how was petrol created? How were gold, silver, iron and other metals among millions of other things made? They were made out of *Paṛam Sañkalps* or divine intentions. Whatever is gross and physical we all can see with our eyes. Everybody else too can see the same thing as we see it. What is not seen is what I want to bring forth. And show you. Distinctive from the five elements, there are energies that are scattered, and if we call out to those energies here and now then this transformation can take place."

"How is it done?" I inquired. I was dying for a smoke. If

ever I make an *Āśrăm* there will be a smoking zone for sure, like there is one at *Avatār Meher Bābā's Āśrăm* at *Meherabad*. Heaven on Earth it is. *Focus Ruz*. "I mean how will this transformation take place; with knowledge, meditation or concentration?"

"Most important is knowledge. Once you are aware, only then a *Niśchay* which means a confirmation or a firm decision comes about."

"But how does one gain knowledge?"

"*Bapuji* will give that to you! He will give you knowledge."

"That is fine, but what if one is in a far away country and in search of knowledge, then what?"

"Then the person will come after he has read the book you are writing."

Either *Mataji* was divinely informed about skills that I didn't know I possessed or very badly misinformed about my ability to spread wisdom. Also I don't agree that knowledge is the sole prerogative of anybody. I believe that if you are seeking something, especially stuff like knowledge, where it involves spreading peace, happiness, wellbeing, or self realization, the Providence, with one's Masters, Arch Angels and the Family of Radiance, will make sure They provide you all the help you need. But the fastest and the best way to seek any knowledge is to go within oneself. Focus on the Breath and ask the Breath to show you the way. Trust me, it is all in the Breath. All the philosophies in the world encompassed within the flow of one's very Breath. That is why meditation or silent contemplation or being centered is so important. I have often found more peace sitting smoking a cigarette, being with the Breath and the name of the Guru, than through all the books I have ever read about spirituality. God is in the Name and the Name eventually is in the Breath. This is my philosophy and my reality. Even after one leaves the body, the spirit continues breathing. One does not stop breathing ever. Yes the spirit breathes more subtle *Prāṇa* or divine energy but the Breath remains. Breath is the essence of life, not just here on planet earth, but it is of essence there too; beyond the beyond. One may not breathe in oxygen but it is another type of *Pṙāṇa* that one breathes. When one evolves on the physical plane, the exhalation becomes slower, till you reach a state where you become one with *Pṙāṇa* and it enters you through the *Crown Chakra*. The Divine Light or Radiance is *Pṙāṇa* of the most subtle kind. We were created from God's Breath. It's all about the Breath! And at this moment I would have willingly cut a politician's left arm to breathe in cigarette smoke. I sighed.

At this point *Bapuji* entered and all of us offered salutations to him. *Bapuji* has mischievous eyes and a smile that lights up his bearded face. He is of medium height and built. It was freezing in Delhi and he had a shawl around his body and a skull-cap covering his head.

We spoke for a few minutes. Tea was organized. *Bapuji* wanted to start-off with the heady stuff first. I wanted to let myself and the reader ease into his philosophy. So, in the following pages I have only retained what I feel is good for mental digestion at such an early time of our journey. By the time the first meeting got over, *Viraf* sat there with a dazed expression, as he found *Bapuji's Hindi* explanation, with the *Sanskrit* words, similar to what one would feel if one strolled into an intergalactic press conference. By the time *Bapuji* had finished, I quickly took off for a quick stroll and did *Pṙāṇāyam* with a few cigarettes.

3

"The world that we know and can see barely equals the tip of an iceberg." *Bapuji* spoke in a clear, soft and in an extremely confident manner. Through the interviews, where he has spoken or voiced his opinion about a number of topics, he spoke as a man who was sure of himself and the knowledge that came through. "So, this creation, in scientific terms is 150-times, 100-crore light years. And the speed of light per second is three-lakh kilometres or one-lakh eighty-six thousand miles. Convert it into a minute, an hour, a day, a month and a year. Compared to our solar galaxy, there are hundred-crore and ten-thousand-crore galaxies that are lakhs-of-times bigger than our galaxy and those galaxies." Began *Bapuji*. "I recently heard that a Sun has been discovered which is a billion times bigger than the Sun of our Solar Galaxy. And in the universe there are innumerable Black holes devouring everything around them. Earlier Black holes did not exist, now they are being created at a rapid pace.

"In our Indian *Śāstṛās* that include the four *Vedas*, sixteen *Upanishads*, eighteen *Puṙāṇas*, two words namely, *Vyakt Duniyā* and *Avyakt Duniyā* which mean Physical World and Ethereal World, are mentioned.

"The first question normally one wants to really know is, who is the Creator or as I call Him, the Almighty Authority? Our *Śāstṛās* have noted that *Brāhṁā* is the Creator, *Viśnu* the Sustainer and *Śiva* the Destroyer. As per the *Gītā* there exist *Anant Koti Brāhṁāṅḍs* or infinite-crore galaxies. Now when you say *Brähmāñḍ*, you refer to a creation of *Brähmā*. So, as there are innumerable *Brähmāñḍs* or Galaxies, logically there have to be as many *Brähmās* or Creators as well. So as there are billions of galaxies, logically there should be billions of *Brähmās, Viśnus* and *Śivas* and equivalent *Devi* Energies; so billions of *Saraswati Mātās* as well!

"What are the tools of science when working with Creation? The tools of science are *Tatva*s or elements. Just like our body is made up of five elements, that are *Ākāś, Vāyu, Agni, Jal* and *Prithvi*, (Ether, Air, Fire, Water and Earth). Water and Earth are heavy by nature. Air and Fire are light in weight. And the element of *Ākāś* or Ether is invisible. Though the element of Ether is invisible, it contains all within itself. It is only within the element of Ether that everything exists. Everything is made of and from this element of Ether. Inside the *Ākāś Tatva* or Ether or as some call it the Space element there is one *Māhā Tatva* or Divine Light.

"How was the world earlier? Earlier, the Almighty had created a world that was *Sampūrna Nirvikāri,* which means that the world was sinless and pure. That means that the world was *Bayhuḍ Nu Paṛam Dhām* which means 'The Supreme Abode of the Infinite' where '*Paṛam*' also means pure. And *Paṛam Ātmās* or Supreme Souls used to inhabit the place.

"What kinds of souls inhabit the world today? Souls were pure then, now they have become impure. Souls that are living today have changed into negative souls or sinful souls. All the *Satya Pradhān Ātmās* or Truth Manifesting or Truth Dominating Souls that existed earlier, were made of the *Paṛam* Light or Divine Light.

"How did creation start? Well the Almighty Authority, created for the first time His *Paṛam Rachnā* or Supreme Creation. He named it the *Paṛam Pitā* or the Founding or

Supreme Father of the Infinite. And then the Founding Father of the Infinite created *Paṛam Ātmās* or the Supreme Souls. Unlike today where the five elements too are polluted, earlier there was the Supreme Element or *Paṛam Tatva*. Inside the *Paṛam Tatva* there is joy and peace; Supreme Joy and Peace.

"So creation started with The Almighty Authority, who was also always present and He created the Founding Father of the Infinite or *Bayhuđ na Paṛam Pitā*. Then through the *Paṛam Pitā* came the *Paṛam Ātmās* or the Supreme Souls. First the *Paṛam Pitā* created out of Himself two Supreme Souls and from these two Supreme Souls were created two more, thus four *Paṛam Ātmās* were generated; then from the four *Paṛam Ātmās* eight *Paṛam Ātmās* came out and then sixteen *Paṛam Ātmās* and in this way the first 108 Supreme Souls were created.

"These 108 gradually formed a circle. Coming together in a ring they formed a spherical sheath on all four sides. This circle had so much power because they had originated directly from the power of the Almighty Authority and had come out of hundred per cent *Paṛam* Light called *Paṛam Pṛakāś*, through the Founding Father. Then from 108 *Paṛam Ātmās*, sixteen-thousand Supreme Souls were created and from them, nine-lakh Supreme Souls were created."

"So from 108 Supreme Souls, nine-lakh Supreme Souls were created?" I inquired.

"Yes, they are *Paṛam, Paṛam, Paṛam Ātmās* or Supreme, Supreme, Supreme Souls. Who is the Almighty Authority? Just like *Jesus Christ* has said: 'I'm the messenger of God and God is Light', similarly the *Śāstṛās* of India reveal, *Pàṛabrāhṁā Pàṛmeśwar Nirākār*… God is Light, God is Light, God is Light…"

"That is also what Prophet *Zarathustra* proclaimed that God is Energy and Light."

"Exactly! The same thing Prophet *Muhammad Sahib*

said, *'Ādam ko Khudā mat kaho; Ādam Khudā nahin; magar Khudā ke noor se Ādam judā nahin'*, when roughly translated: Don't call Adam God; Adam is not God; But from the Light of God, Adam is not separate.

"I am a soul. You are a soul. I am not the body. You are not the body. This is basic knowledge. We have forgotten all *Ātmà Swarūp Nu Jñān* or the knowledge of the soul-form and believe the body to be all. And we have begun to believe the five-elemental world to be the be-all and end-all of everything. Caught in the five-elemental body, we have started to look at each other as bodies."

"And forgotten the greatest reality that I am the spirit, I am That, *Aum Tat Sat*."

"Exactly *betā*. *Aum Tat Sat*. If you see yourself as a body, you will see everything in the physical aspect. If we remain in the *Ātmà Swarūp* and see each other as souls or spirits or *Ātmās*, then that is when we shall have *Ātmà Swarūp Nu Jñān* or the Knowledge of the Image of the Soul-form. The moment we see and recognize each other as His Creation and a part of Him that is when we will have the *Divya Swarūp Nu Jñān* or Knowledge of the Divine Self. That is when the recorded knowledge from the soul starts to emerge. All the soul has ever experienced, in its entire journey, from creation up to now, is revealed.

"The very first creation that the Almighty Authority created, we call Him the *Bayhuđ Na Paṛam Pitā* or The Supreme Father of the Infinite. *Brähṁā* of this World is only called *Paṛam Pitā*. If we wish to differentiate between the Founding Father and *Brähṁā*, then the former is the Infinite *Brähṁā*, while *Brähṁā* of our galaxy is the Finite *Brähṁā*. And Who is the creator of the Founding Father of the Infinite? It is the Almighty Authority. The Almighty Authority does nothing. He is *Akartā*, which means a non-doer. He gets work done. Through whom does He get His work done? Through the *Bayhuđ Na Paṛam Pitā* or the Supreme Father of the Infinite. The Supreme Father of the Infinite has to create or compose, as that is the Will of the Almighty Authority. He has within Him all the power and everything – He is the Power House. And what is the Power? The Power is the First Pure Divine Light, the *Paṛam Pṛakāś*. The creations that come off the *Paṛam Pṛakāś* will ultimately claim energy from the Almighty Authority. So, taking the power from the Power House, The Supreme Father of the Infinite created the Infinite First Pure Souls; the First 108 Souls."

"So the first 108 souls who came from the Creator are the main foundation? But actually it should be 109, as The Absolute Authority created first the Supreme Father of the Infinite?" I asked.

"Yes but the 108 souls came from the Supreme Father of the Infinite. Then through the first 108, sixteen thousand were created and more and more were created. So, yes, the first 108 souls are the main Master Creators of the Total Creation. If we catch hold of the 108, then we can bring peace and harmony in creation. From 108 *Ātmās*, eventually came about nine-lakh souls. Thus, each time souls were created, the power in them kept declining. Nine lakh souls claimed less power from the Power House. Because when from one soul another soul comes out, there is a friction that takes place and since all this is taking place where only the Supreme Divine Radiance or *Paṛam* Light exists, the friction caused the *Paṛam* Light to create the *Paṛam Tatva*s *or* pure prime elements. So, how was the *Vāyu Mandàḷ* or atmosphere there? It was made of *Paṛam Tatva*s or pure prime elements.

"Today, you exist in the world of five elements that is why your body is of five elements. If you want to travel to other planets or another world, for example, you wish to travel to Saturn or Jupiter, then you would have to make your body comprise of elements that exist there."

Bapuji then went into greater detail and a lot of stuff flew way-way-way above my head. I saw *Viraf* staring straight through *Bapuji*, as living in America for over twenty-five years, his *Hindi* and *Sanskrit* had become slightly rusted.

I wanted to smile. I wanted to smoke. I wanted to fill my body with nicotine *Tatva.*

Then mercifully somebody entered with a tray of cups and the aroma of liquid nicotine called by many as tea greeted the nostrils. I got a call from the Supreme *Tatva,* known to most men, as the wife. She informed me that my daughter, *Meher* wanted to know why I had not taken her with me when writing the book. I spoke to *Meher* in *Gujarati.* I tried to explain to her that it would be difficult for me to interview *Bapuji,* as when with her she made it a point that I didn't interact with men, women, or any of the five elements of nature. She told me a few things best left unpublished.

After I disconnected the phone, we spoke for a while. It was getting really cold.

"You speak *Gujarati*?" *Bapuji* inquired, as we left the hall. He was genuinely happy. "That's very good. From henceforth we will speak in *Gujarati.*" He beamed like a small child who had found his favourite toy.

I approached *Viraf.* He smiled.

"After a point, the Hindi got so complicated I could have been sitting in front of a man speaking traditional Chinese."

4

Meher my youngest child was barely four-and-a-half years old when these interviews were taking place with *Bapuji.* As a large part of my day was spent in interviews and the latter-half of the day spent in channelling, her opinion about Delhi, *Bapuji* and all those who came to meet me wasn't exactly, for a want of a better word, *kosher*.

After breakfast, we would roam about the hotel premises, which was rather extensive and we would play in the garden.

"Daddy I have noticed you are not spending time with me in Delhi." She spoke without looking at me. She was trying to chase this frog that seemed to have an aversion for social interaction.

"You know I write books, sweetheart."

"Why do you have to write books? Nobody reads books Daddy. They all watch television."

"Yeah I know and what have I taught you about television?"

"That television is more interesting than people."

"Good girl of mine."

"But why *doos* you have to go to work? Why *doos* you have to write books. Stay with me?"

"Ok first and foremost it's not *doos*. The right word is 'do', there's no word called *doos* in the Queen's language…"

"The Queen is an idiot. *Doos* is a good word. You stay with me here and play. I miss you. Why can't *Bapuji* speak to you on the phone? And what is this book about?"

"The book is about God and how everybody can become one with God and become God. Wouldn't you like to become one with God or become God yourself?"

"God means like *Šivji* and *Kṛiṣna*?"

"Yes."

"And demons mean *Mahisasur* and *Raktabēj*… who *Mā Duṛgā* and *Mā Kāli* killed?"

"Yup…see, each one of us has the potential or the power to become like God or the demon, and often every day, we become sometimes like God and sometimes like Monsieur *Raktabēj*, so who would you want to become; God or demon?"

She looked up at me. Squinted as the morning sun beams fell on her eyes, and also highlighted her brown hair and her little button like nose.

"I don't want to become like God or demon, I am happy being a human being."

I couldn't help but laugh aloud. That was the wisest answer anybody had given me ever.

"What gave you the idea that you are a human being? Last night you remember you threw your milk bottle on my head…."

"But why *doos* Daddy have to go to work. Today you send mummy to write the book."

"Ya sure. If I send your mother, your mother will be speaking and poor *Bapuji* will be writing another book."

She began to giggle.

"That is true. Hee hee."

An hour later, after assuring *Meher* that I would get many surprises for her, I left once again to interview *Bapuji*. Delhi true to its promise continued chilling my bone marrow. I met *Mataji*, *Anant* and *Sakshi*. We sat once again in the meditation hall where the temperature was a few degrees lower. I put on my thug cap and we sat in a circle. Tea and biscuits were served. I insisted that I would have to write the book in a manner that even a person not really clued onto spirituality could grasp otherwise we would have about fourteen people reading the book and seven people understanding it.

Bapuji was in his room. I was to be taken there later. He rarely came out of the room. He meditated and contemplated in the room all alone. That's the perk of being a Sage. People leave you alone. If I told my family I wanted to sit in the room and be left alone, from the security guard standing outside at the colony gate to my daughter, all would take it as a mission to make sure my room resembled *Churchgate* station at peak hour. Anyway back to *Bapuji,* he ate one meal a day which he consumed around two in the afternoon. If hungry, he would have some tea, or soup or salad later. He only came out of the room if he had to travel, or if he had to meet somebody who couldn't make it to the *Āśrăm*.

"*Betā,* what is knowledge? Who is the giver of knowledge?" *Mataji* looked at me waiting for an answer. I smiled back. "As they say: *Kāl ke panje se chudao; hey Mā Ashta Bhavani,* which means: Please release me from the clutches of *Kāl*, O Mother *Ashta Bhavāni*. So, how will the whole world get free from the clutches of time? And do you wish to free the world and be free from its clutches and not keep on spinning in the circle of *Kāl? Kāl* means death. *Kāl* means time. Do you want to release the whole world from the clutches of *Kāl*? So then first of all you have to realize how one frees oneself from the clutches of *Kāl*.

"*Bapuji* taught me how we came from the *Amar Lok* that is the Immortal World to the *Mrutyu Lok,* the World of Death. See now – space, time and speed of each place is different. What it was last year it is not now. What will be there in the next year is not today and would not have been last year as well. I want to tell you that if you want to free the world from the clutches of *Kāl*, then this is the only time that you can free the world. Take the revolving fan as an example. When the speed of the fan is slow you can see the blades, but faster the speed, the blades become virtually a blur. So, similarly, we cannot see time. Whatever indications the *Śāstṛās* have shown, whatever is happening in the world is right in front of all. From one mango seed an entire mango tree comes about. From that one mango tree that you have planted you can get hundreds of mangoes over the years. Then you plant a hundred seeds and over the years thousands of mangoes come about, which means thousands of seeds, which means the potential of thousands of more mango trees and then you get a lakh seeds and from the lakh seeds that you plant you get crores of mangoes. You plant a crore seeds and you get trillions of mangoes and so on and so forth.

"But it all began with one seed. But tell me one thing, as many seeds that came… where did they get their basic power from? What was their source? The source was from the first mango seed that was planted into Mother Earth. And who would have the complete knowledge of all the seeds?

"The One who planted that first seed but through centuries, the potency of the forthcoming seeds keep getting depleted isn't it?" I inquired.

"Exactly! Mankind today is not as agile, pure and strong as mankind was centuries ago. Our food is contaminated with fertilizers and pesticides residual. Today the kids lack joy and agility. Why is it so? Because the elements that had power previously do not have power anymore, that's why our kids do not have life or *Jān*. Their minds are sharp, but their bodies are not agile."

"But the kids of today are far more intelligent and perceptive than we were as kids. Kids a few decades ago were rather slow and daft when compared to this new batch of wailing monsters!" I added my two bit. I am sort of a pro where kids are concerned.

"That is because the elements of Water and Earth have increased and the other elements have decreased. With the increase of Water and Earth elements, the kids will be smarter for material and worldly things than what their parents and grand-parents were. The percentage of the *Tatvas* of *Jal* and *Dhàṛti* is about 96.999%. It is the heaviness of our body. And point 001% is the strength of our soul, due to which we are alive. *Ātmā,* the soul is also a power".

"The power of our soul is only so much? ...point 001% only!!...? From where did you derive this percentage?"

"This *Bapuji* has revealed. When *Bapuji* goes into *Yog* or deep meditation whatever he sees he reveals to us. Also, as I have told you before, *Bapuji* says that this percentage is also to help one to understand the distribution of elements and also the loss of power of elements from the start up to now. If we go backwards in time, the population around 240 years ago was just fifty-crore people. Imagine the power the soul had then as the elements of Ether, Air and Fire were far more than what we have now."

"The body has five elements I have understood but what is the soul made up of? How many elements make the soul?"

"*Ātmā* is made up of *Paṛam Tatva* or the Supreme Element and *Paṛam Pṛakāś* which means Divine Light. So this component is getting lesser. Why it's getting lesser is because with more of our wants, wishes and *Sañkalps* emerging out of us, the power of our soul is getting weakened and this is the reality of life! Whatever we think happens. If not us, then someone else makes it happen. But it happens for sure. Our *Sañkalps* do not go to waste. Ok let's go 5200 years, during the time of *Kṛiṣna Avatār*."

"Ok off we go 5200 years ago."

"Here what did we have, what was the constitution of our body? We had forty-five per cent Ether, Air and Fire or *Ākāś, Vāyu and, Agni*; fifty-three per cent Water and land; and two per cent energy of the soul.

"Though fifty-three per cent comprised of Water and land, but the important thing is forty-five per cent of our body was made of Ether, Air and Fire; elements that are very light. With such an elemental break up the body was so light that anybody with the right spiritual attitude and power could easily fly and gravity did not have a hold over that individual. The bodies were light. And this also means that the earth was light. The land, earth or *Dhàṛti* too was light. Oh, so weightless, the world was!"

"When you say the earth was weightless, you mean the laws of gravity were different?"

"Yes. Vehicles could fly as is written in the *Ramayana* and the *Gītā*. When a Sage with intent stomped his foot on the ground, water would spurt out – that means that the earth too was light. So, what does that mean? *Hanumānji* could fly, *Kṛiṣna* could fly. So when the elements within us have less Water and Earth, the body is light, and the lighter the body, the soul energy too is stronger. You know the famous *Chaṇakya....* He used to walk extremely long distances to teach. How did he manage that? There weren't cars in those days but he could walk miles and miles every day to reach his destination. Our ancestors would walk twenty-five kilometers on foot and would not tire. Why? What was different then and now? They were big built but the body elements were light. Time, speed and space, as I had previously explained are different at different places. What was there last year, is not here today, what is present now, will not be there one year hence. Our elements are getting heavier now."

"*Bapuji* has come here to give a message. What message has he come to give? That if we go through a transformation or change, it is better, and through meditation one can make the elements within us light. Ok take *Kṛiṣna Avatār* for instance. It is known that He had sixteen thousand one hundred and eight wives. That logically means He had taken on sixteen thousand, one hundred and eight forms; He had one manifestation of Himself for one queen."

"Why in God's name did He want so many wives?" I inquired.

"That I will tell you later…"

"No, no, no. I want to know this now. Focus on *Kṛiṣna*'s sixteen-thousand, one-hundred-and-eight wives please."

"He had so many wives for a reason."

"Trust me there wasn't, isn't and will never be a reason good enough to have so many wives."

This is what I have found out from the 21st century's Supreme *Taŧva*, commonly called *Google*. Lord *Kṛiṣna* killed a demon named *Bhaumasura*. Our chap *Bhaumasura*, for some reason, I will never be able to fathom, had kidnapped thousands of princess and held them captive in his palace. The real estate market must have been really down or *Bhaumasura* must have been wickedly rich to accommodate over sixteen thousand princesses in one palace. So Lord *Kṛiṣna* killed our chap and when Lord *Kṛiṣna* entered the palace, the princesses had one look at Him and fell in love with Him. Also in those days if a woman was even touched by another man nobody would accept the woman as his wife. So Lord *Kṛiṣna* took it upon Himself to manifest Himself sixteen-thousand, one-hundred-and-eight-times to marry each and every princess. It is also mentioned that each of these princesses were in reality manifestations of *Mā Laxmi*. I paid attention to *Mataji*.

"It is all about determination. The determination to transform and increase the energy of the soul and *Paṛam Taŧvas* will eventually make you become light and finally go back to your source. Even if you have an as-thin-as-a-strand-of-hair less determination, then we ourselves are responsible for not reaching The Source. We don't have to live for three hundred years but live to bring about change and transform the world. Make the world *Pṛakāśmai* or enlightened or bring light to the world."

"Ok so your creator may not be the Supreme Creator but could be one of the 108 Seed Souls. So basically the souls go back first to their original source and after all is assimilated that original source goes back to the Founding Father of the Infinite and then merge into the Absolute Authority."

"Yes. Say you are one of the first 108 Souls. Now from you hundreds of thousands of souls would have come about; as from you many of the thousands of souls in the first sixteen-thousand souls originated and then from you many of those nine-lakh souls originated and then from those many of the two-crore souls originated. So all those who came from you will first merge back into you and then you will merge back into the Creator who will then merge into the Absolute Authority." Explained both *Anant* and *Sakshi*, in their own way.

"Ok, that makes sense. But we have through our *Sañkalps* or desires created innumerable creations. So when will they all merge? Also they should want to merge isn't it?" I inquired.

"Don't they say that the gates of *Swarg* or heaven are always open? But transformation can come about only if you have the will and the knowledge. But the fact is that after leaving the body I will not be able to do much for the benefit of the world. But in this body I can sit and perform *Yog*, and work for the benefit of the world that I cannot do after I leave the world."

"Is that the reason they say that the body is most important?"

"Yes! What is this life? What is said in the *Gurbāni* – The Holy Book of the Sikh community – I do not know much of what the Sikh Holy Book says but *Akāl Puṛakh, Akāl Takht; Akāl Mooṛt*", where *Akāl* means, That which *Kāl* or time and death cannot eat up. *Akāl Puṛakh* is being timeless and deathless; *Takht* is The Throne of the Timeless and Deathless One and *Akāl Mooṛt* is the changeless form. One needs to go beyond *Kāl or* time to be truly immortal. If I stay in the five elements, then *Kāl* will eat me up. If I want to save myself from being eaten up by *Kāl*, then I will have to go to being in the Form of Light – I'll have to see the enlightened-version or the *Pṛakāś Swarūp* of me, then *Kāl* will not be able to enter me. In case I have my *Pṛakāś Swarūp* then *Kāl* will not be able to come close to me...."

"Even when you are in the body *Kāl* will not be able to touch you, if you get connected and constantly be aware of your lightened spirit body... is that what you are saying?" That's me again.

"Yes, that is right. That's what I wanted you to realize. Okay, now you have gone 5200 years back... and just imagine that you have a body that constitutes large portion of your five-elemental structure comprising of Ether, Air and Fire or *Ākāś, Vāyu and Agni*. How must your body be then? You will be the proud owner of a *Känchän Kāyā* that is crystal-clear body, right? So when you have more of Ether, Air and Fire that is *Ākāś, Vāyu and Agni* in you, you will be calm and in a meditative state. The more we are in the state of Ether, the calmer we are. Because we have less of Ether or *Ākāś* that is when we think more and we indulge ourselves more in the world."

"And when we get more entangled in the world, then karma increases and the karmic play never ever ends. And all this was around five-thousand two-hundred years before *Christ*?"

"Yes son. Around the time of *Zarathustra*, the Prophet

of your religion, *Zoroastrianism*; as you must know that Prophet *Zarathustra* was before even *Kṛiṣna Avatār*. The higher the level of souls the fewer in number they will be. Look at the kind of noble work your community and those who follow your religion are involved in from the beginning of time. Now these people also will have a Seed Soul, am I correct? The One who established the religion will be The Seed."

"Prophet *Zarathustra*."

"Yes. He *will* be there. Then won't He come here? It could well be any one of you. The One who has established your religion only will listen to the cries of those who were, are and will and those with Him? He will have to come and listen and bring about transformation? Who else would do that? The One who is the seed only will bring about change in each soul belonging to that seed and His religion. Your religion is the first established religion. *Zarathustra* is the first known Prophet. Though *Śrī Ram* came much before Prophet *Zarathustra*, *Śrī Ram* was not a Prophet but an *Avatār* and Hinduism is not a religion but a way of life. All religions that came after Zoroastrianism, which *betā* is your religion came from the Prime Seed.

"So now back to the lightness of the body. Those days the energy of the soul was high. If the soul's energy is two per cent, Ether and Light element is more, then if the need be we could fly. Just like when one is acting in a play, one takes on the personality of the character portrayed, similarly, when we come into the body of five elements, we tend to forget our true selves and believe in the character we are living. Where do we come from? Who are we? What are we? It is all within, but we are oblivious of our true self and identity. We end up believing only in the five elements. Anyway, as I was telling you that we had an extremely light body earlier. The population then was barely eight crore. The *Zoroastrian* religion came into being and can you imagine what it must have been during *Śrī Ram's* time when the population was far smaller."

"Which year did *Śrī Ram* come on earth?"

"We are told almost 8,69,000 years ago." Informed *Sakshi*.

"He was before *Kṛiṣna Avatār* thus in the *Treytā Yug*." *Anant* replied.

"That is the story of this *Brāhmāñḍ betā*. *Śrī Ram* had come to give a message just like *Kṛiṣna*, and *Christ*, even *Guru Nanak* came and gave the message of *Ek Omkār* and said: *Akāl Puṛakh, Akāl Takht, Akāl Mooṛt* which means that which is beyond the power of *Kāl* or time and death. If one is not beyond *Kāl*, then however powerful one may be, be it a Sage, a *Rūśimuni or a Tapasvi*, *Kāl* will devourer that one eventually."

"Ok so I understand that the five elements are making us heavy and we need to get closer to our true form. How does one do that?"

"Now listen carefully: whenever you close your eyes, imagine your inner body and external body to be made of light, and believe yourself to be made of light and one day you will actually see yourself filled with light, that's when you will have a body of light. Keep increasing the light; keep imagining yourself glowing more and more with this light. This is the way you go about becoming light. Everything is in the *Sañkalp* or the thought, intention. The world was made out of thoughts. It's all about the power of thought. Believe something and slowly you will become that thing."

"You mean go back to our original form of becoming light once again, as we all have come from the Great Light?"

"Yes. And you remember everything started with the First Seed. Even smaller than the mustard seed is the seed of a banyan tree. And the roots of that banyan tree are so deep and spread out being really long, miles and miles long. Tell me how will you find the seed in that? You will not be able to find it, right? The seed has been dissipated or disseminated inside the tree. All the strength, power and everything that was there has been spread: *'Hey Arjun, yeh Sruśti ek ulta vruksh hai, aur Main upar mein Ek Beej hun'*, means, 'Oh *Arjun*, the whole of creation is an upside down tree and I am the seed on the top'. So who was the One who said *'Main'* or 'I'. The One who said 'I am the One Up There at the top', was the one who had sent *Kṛiṣna* making him a messenger of Himself. Just like we tell our kids, 'go *betā* do this work and come'. Where have we come from? Who are we? What were our powers? Why have we lost our powers? Where did our strengths go and how will we collect our energies back? How will we go back to that Original State? This is all possible if we meditate and infuse ourselves with the Light. More the light element and space element the more we shall strengthen our soul and slowly gain back our power. That is the only way the world can be liberated from pain and sadness. One may get some peace and happiness for an hour or two after we meet a holy person. But that *Sukh* and *Ṣanti* – peace and joy is not permanent. Even *Śrī Ram*, did He find happiness? No He did not. First He was exiled. Then *Mā Sita* was taken away from Him by *Ravana*. Then He had to send *Mā* away from Himself and His kingdom. After that His own children attacked His army. Then *Mā Sita* took *Prithvi Samādhi,* where she prayed to Mother Earth, and the earth opened and she stepped within and the earth closed on Her. She entered the earth, to prove Her innocence and also preserve Her self-respect. So *Śrī Ram,* I don't think had a very happy life." *Mataji* emphasized.

"Yes." I agreed. This is true. I had just read that

eventually *Śrī Ram*, entered the water and took *Jal Samādhi or* Water Liberation, which in other words, if you look at it, *Śrī Ram* ended His life by walking into the water and not coming out. I sighed. Life is an exercise in futility. Nobody comes out of it sane, happy or alive. What was God thinking when He created mankind? Or more profoundly, what was He smoking when He created mankind?

"*Kṛiṣna* too found no happiness?" *Mataji* continued. "No. He did not. So in this world of five elements no one will ever find continuous happiness or perpetual peace. You may have all the money in the world, but a constant state of happiness is not to be got. The only way one can get perpetual happiness is by becoming the Light. Think and believe that inside you there is a Light Form. Assert: 'I am the Light; Awaken the Light within Me'. Slowly you will become that Light. And then *Kāl* will not eat you up. Remember the prayer, *Oh Mā Ashta Bhavani, please release me from the clutches of Time. Ashta* means The One who brings all eight powers with Her to release all from the clutches of *Kāl* or time and death. But this is achieved through constant practice. If possible sit in front of the sun, so as you sit in front of the sun, your light body will emerge. Once you have caught it and once you have seen it, then you will see it over and over again. That is why you who are *Parsis* or *Zoroastrians* worship the Sun. Then up above, 'beyond the element of Ether' or 'beyond the Skies' or *Ākāś se Pareh* even beyond the 150 *Arab* or trillion light-years away, we have to go there with our intellect and create one *Rūp* or image of ours. We have to create a satellite of our body."

"And that *Rūp* or body will remain there."

"Yes. So now you will create this body? It has to be done by oneself with one's thoughts and prayers and meditation. And after emerging there it will supply you power here. And through that your vibrations will reach out to the whole world. And all those souls that are connected with your soul will come forth like magnets. So, someone or the other will become a medium? A medium will be created. Like how you came here today. So someone or another will become a medium, the harbinger or bringer of Light. Haven't you felt that very often when you are channelling *Bābā's* energy, there are many others hearing His message apart from those sitting in the body in front of you?"

I nodded. Yes, have felt this very often in the channelling room. I remember the first time I realized this was nearly a decade prior. I was in a farm house near *Mumbai,* with *Mr.* and *Mrs. Mehta.* It was at night, and they were asking me questions and I was there but not there, if you know what I mean…, and suddenly for some weird reason, I got this impression that the room was filled with people, who I could sense but not see. Then *Mr. Mehta* looked at me and said: 'Why do I feel that we are not the only three people in this room. That the whole room is full of people we cannot see right now.' Since then I have often felt that there were many more chaps listening in, may be curious or just astral bums, passing their time.

"How does one achieve liberation?" continued *Mataji. Bapuji* says that there is *Mukti* and *Jēvan Mukti. Mukti* means the merger of the soul into the One from which it has originated. It means to merge into the *Dhàṛma* Guru or The Teacher, whosoever it is. That's *Mukti. Jēvan Mukti* means that while still alive, our body will be made of *Amrut Taŧva* or Eternal Element, that it will be made of *Paṛam Pṛakāś* or Supreme Eternal Light during our physical time on earth. The *Devatās* or Gods too have a body of three elements only. In *Indra Lok,* the King of *Devatās, Indra* too is worried whether someone would take away His kingdom, rule and power. That is because only when in the physical body can you truly reach that eternal state of Oneness, as when in the spirit body you can reach what your karmas and thoughts in the physical body have generated. Progress is very slow in the spirit world."

"So what you are trying to say is that only when you are in the physical body, you can determine where you are going to be in the spirit body and thus the all pervading importance of being a human being. We determine where we are going to be in the spirit plane when we are in the gross physical body and if we are to merge with the Creator, it can only be decided when in the physical body, not in the spirit body?"

Both *Anant* and *Sakshi* nodded in the affirmative.

"We do all here-and-now and bear all here-and-now and finish it all here-and-now. All accounts *hisāb-kitāb* for the now. Now we are alive for others and the world. The only true purpose of life should be to bring about a positive change in the complete universe. If you *will* it, then truly this whole world will change. What is the meaning of *Avatār*? Even Lord *Kṛiṣna* said rightly: 'Oh *Arjun*, I do not go into the womb of my mother. My birth is divine and I come as one who is *Avatārit*' which means I appear or I simply Emerge. *Kṛiṣna*'s *Rūp* was *Avatārit* from up there. In the womb of the mother was only the body but he did not enter it", informed *Mataji*.

"After the formation of the five-elemental body, and when it was ready and delivered, it is then that *Kṛiṣna*'s soul just entered into the body and not while it was inside the womb of the mother", added *Sakshi*.

"When *Kṛiṣna* was six months old, He killed *Pūtnā*, a *rākśasa*, He killed *Shishupāl*, *Jarāsangh*, He killed so many *asurās* or animal-like evil creatures", added *Mataji*.

"*Kṛiṣna* used to kill by just His look. How would He kill? *Kṛiṣna* would never use a weapon; He would just look into the eyes of the person and pull out the soul from their bodies. Similarly, the moment one feels that 'I am doing this', that 'I am giving knowledge', that 'I did this great work', we fall into the trap of ego or *Ahañkār* and that's when it will kill us. Among all other vices or evils like anger, greed, desires, *Ahañkār* or pride is the most dangerous. I am nothing. I believe that I am zero. Why did only *Arjun* have *Divya Druśti* or Divine Vision or why was only He given that vision? '*Arjun, tu mujhe inhi ākhoñ say nahiñ dekh saktā; Main tujhe Divya Druśti detā hun, usey tu Mujhe dekh, usey tu Mujhe jān*'. 'O *Arjun*, you cannot see me with your earthly eyes, so I am giving you Divine Vision, with that you see me; know me.' Son, Divine Vision, one can only glimpse for a few seconds. I have seen it but for a second and I caught it and still keep it within me and that is the *Paṛam* Truth, the Supreme Truth. That is what I want to show you and through you I want to give it to the world. And on *Bapuji's* wisdom I have complete faith. Otherwise, in India, the culture that I come from, traditional, orthodox culture, no woman would leave her home and family."

"So when did you meet *Bapuji*?" I inquired.

"I had already left my home many times before but would always return in a few days or weeks but once I met *Bapuji* I never returned. And it was in search of these questions that he gave me answers one by one. But initially whenever he gave me knowledge, the three elemental bodies would not allow me to listen to him. I would not be allowed to listen with focus. I'm telling you, I would be sitting and everybody would be listening and I would not understand anything at all."

"You mean the spirits wouldn't let you grasp anything?"

"They would not allow me to understand anything. Make my attention wander off to some other place; sometimes my mind would become dull. But *Bapuji* was sure and had faith that this was the only energy who would be able to understand the knowledge he wanted to impart and it was *Bapuji's* decision and faith in me, that gave me the confidence to continue. So, there was only one thing that I understood clearly: that this entire world of five elements that we see can brighten up and get enlightened with Pure Light if we all work towards it. This is what I grasped and held on to. And slowly *Bapuji's* teachings began to enter my consciousness and I began to understand all. I have great respect and reverence for *Bapuji*. I knew that other than this person no one else in this world would be able to give the Knowledge. From that very day, I decided and had faith that *Bapuji* gives knowledge to liberate one from *Mrutyu Kāl*, the Clutches of Death and Karma. And no one else can impart that knowledge. It was on the basis of this one thing that I understood about Pure Light that made me firmly decide. It was on the basis of this one thing that I found my faith and then the knowledge started to emerge. *Bapuji* would give talks and he would teach a lot of people, it was not that I had a special class or something. I too listened to him in the crowd. How can we liberate the world from the clutches of time? Everybody keeps on chanting the *Māhā Mrityunjay Mantra*, but is anyone saved? No one is! What is the meaning of *Mrityunjay*? It means Victory over Death. By just saying your *mantras* nothing happens."

Ok, I have a serious issue. I am a firm believer in *Nām Smàraṇ* or chanting the name of one's Lord and Master. I have seen miracles take place. Calamities averted. Death stalled. Illness cured. Suffering mitigated to the minimum. Life enhanced. Mental, emotional, physical, spiritual, financial, medical, legal and other imbalances rectified or quality of life enhanced but just simple chanting your *Mantra*. Whatever the *Mantra* may be and in which ever language chanted, firm faith, complete positive surrender, absolute unquestionable faith and most essential and of complete paramount importance, absolute mad love for whoever you pray to, can move mountains. Chant your *Mantra* to such a degree that when while asleep you turn at night and your sleep breaks for that fraction of a second, the *Mantra* begins. Merge with your *Mantra*. Become one with the *Mantra*. And then the *Mantra* will first burn away all your karmas and take you where your Master, Lord, Goddess, wants you to reach.

Also the literal meaning of the *Māhā Mrityunjay Mantra* means victory over death. But according to me, It means the victory from the fear of death; liberation from the fear of death. And I have seen this *Mantra* work. Often during channelling, *Sai* of *Shirdi*, has asked those who come to Him, to perform the recital of the *Mantra* for a particular number of days, to either help the ailing person to recover or then be released from the suffering, and I have seen It work, every time. This is my experience and the experiences of innumerable folks who have listened to *Bābā Sai* during channelling and done the needful. Often the illness remains but the individual suffering from that particular ill ease or disease, doesn't feel the pain. Of course I am nobody to argue with Sages but this is just my point of view. *Back to Mataji.*

"So, now how do we change and transform the whole world? We do not wish that people scream or cry and bombs explode, or fights take place and the world submerges into water. This has taken place *Anant-Koti* or innumerable crore times. How will you save the world? How will you save all the people? It can be done only through knowledge, *betā*. It is only through the right knowledge that one can become immortal. And you must emerge your body of Light and never ever make a *Sañkalp* that you want to leave your body. Never ever desire to leave your body *betā*. I know you have an issue being in the physical body but you must understand that it is only while in this body you can make a difference. Instead, affirm: 'Within and with this body I have to transform the whole world and the *Anant Koti Brāhṁāñḍs* or the crores of galaxies. I have to lighten and enlighten the entire World. I have to spread the light.' That is our work. And if this Light comes… then how will this whole world become? It will become *Amar Lok* – a place where there is no limit of age and limitation of birth and death. We will be only in our Divine Forms and we will not be aware of the difference between male and female. We are aware of the differences of sex only in this world of five elements; otherwise there is no awareness of the difference. One is a union of male and female even in the body. But what a mother can say a father can't and what a father can do a mother can't. As a mother I can tell you anything and you will keep quiet. You might not keep quiet with a man. So that's why I am here as a woman, a man would not be able to tell you like that. With the father, a son or daughter may not be able to talk freely but with the mother one can talk anything. Also the mother can talk to you anyhow and you will keep quiet. And where will you get the power of purity? Only from the mother right? Till the time the child is in the lap of the mother, till then the child does not think about anything going wrong, till then he or she doesn't want anything, but when the child is out of her lap, the child wants all and everything. So the strength of purity one can get only from the mother. You say *Mā* and you start receiving. What type of mother? The *Mā* who imparts Divine Powers and Divine *Śaktis* and Energies is the *Mā*. The Mother who will impart me with Divine Knowledge, The Mother who will make me *Amar*, Immortal and Forever; that's why in front of the Mother, nothing happens to the child. The child is safe. And the one who says *Mā* has already got the *Amar Tatva;* you should never ever think that you want to leave your body. You have to – with this body only – transform and bring about change in this world. It is such a huge responsibility. Now take yourself, you are born on *Kāli Chaudas*, which means you are born on the most auspicious night of *Mā Kāli* and the most auspicious day of *Mā Laxmi*. So, who is *Kāli*?

When Her children come in front of Her, She is the mother who takes away all their negativity that is within them. *Kāli* has an instrument called the *Khapad*, in Her hands that She uses to take away the negativity of all Her children. What does *Mā Kāli* do after taking all the negativity? She does *Swāhā* of it and all that negativity changes into *Amrut* or Nectar of Immortality. From poison, it becomes *Amrut*. So after removing all negativity from Her children, She makes Her children pure. Nothing but purity remains. Just like a mother gives a bath and washes and loves a child like that in a similar way it is a *Jñān Sñān*, a bath of knowledge."

5

My phone kept ringing. I noticed I had got twenty missed calls from the same number. Who would call me twenty times and still not take the hint that maybe I just could not take the call or had left this five-elemental body and had got astral wings on my three elemental astral posterior. I of course needed to fill myself up with nicotine *Taṭva* badly too. So I excused myself. I walked out of the *Āśrăm* and sat on a rock under a tree and lit a cigarette. The phone rang again. The phone showed the number of the same persistent caller.

"Yes. Who is this?" On the other end of the line, was a lady who had come for channelling with her family often. She was from Mumbai and had driven down to *Pune* with her family on innumerable occasions. Now, she, along with her family, was in Delhi too. Could she come with her family as there were very grave issues that needed *Bābā's* guidance? "Ok, can you make it at two thirty tomorrow?" She said sure, two thirty, tomorrow, could I message the address of the home I would be channelling in? I said ok I would. I switched off the phone and smoked in peace. My head was reeling. How would I write this book I wondered? All this stuff was so different from my concept of spirituality. But I knew this book was needed as had been contemplating a book on Oneness but in the fiction format, like *The Fakir* books. The phone rang again. It was the same caller. Now what?

"Yes?"

"You have given us the time for tomorrow."

"Yes two thirty."

"Is it two thirty in the morning or afternoon?"

I shut my eyes. I so desperately wanted exit out of this five elemental body, as was certain there would be no phones at least in heaven or hell. I assumed even in hell there was a certain level of mercy on its inhabitants.

"You can come at two-thirty at night. I will see you at two-thirty in the afternoon." I switched off the phone.

Muttering words that were left best unpublished I entered the *Āśrăm*.

Along with *Mataji*, *Sakshi* and *Anant*, I walked up the stairway to meet *Bapuji*. I looked around the *Āśrăm* with greater interest. If I were to ever channel at two-thirty at night, I would have to come and settle down in this *Āśrăm* for good.

I entered the room and *Bapuji* got out of bed and gave me a warm hug. The room was a simple one with a large bed and a television in front of it with wide windows to the left of the room and a bathroom door. Not a very large room. Not too small either. Depends which city you have grown up in. If in Mumbai the room was nice and big. If in Delhi, it was a small cozy room. If in *Pune* it was just the right size.

"You wanted to know how we have come on this earth." *Sakshi* spoke softly. "*Mataji* sometimes says *Paṛam Taŧva* and sometimes *Paṛam* Light, which at times gets you confused. What we see here on earth is the replica of the subtle world. Earlier there was *Paṛam Pṛakāś* or Divine Light (I would like to think of it as *Supreme Divine Radiance*. So henceforth when we talk of *Paṛam Pṛakāś* or *Supreme Divine Radiance* it means one and the same). Initially there were no elements. The five-elemental beings came into existence only at a very later stage. The Supreme Divine

Radiance *or Paṛam Pṛakāś* is not a *Taṫva* or an element. It is pure Energy or *Śakti.* The Absolute Authority is made up of only *Paṛam Pṛakāś.* Though the Founding Father of the Infinite was created by *Paṛam Pṛakāś*, the process of creation created within the Founding Father of the Infinite a marginal loss of the *Supreme Divine Radiance* and the first *Paṛam, Paṛam, Paṛam Taṫva* was created, which is the *Paṛam, Paṛam, Paṛam Ākāś Taṫva* or Purest of the Purest of the Pure Ether Element or Space Element. Thus even *Paṛam Taṫva*s, be it Ether, Air, Fire, were Supreme Elemental Bodies."

"So basically in this stage there is only Supreme Radiance which may have a hint of Divine Ether, Wind and Fire elements?"

"It is a vacuum that is made of the three elements; Space, Air and Fire. But you still are not in the astral world. The astral world is purely three-elemental where the elements of Ether, Air and Fire have less and less of the Supreme Divine Radiance till you reach the five-elemental world where there is virtually no *Paṛam Pṛakāś*, barely any *Paṛam Taṫva*s but nearly all of normal five elements. If I have to talk of today, then I am in a five-elemental body. I have to do great *Tapasyā* that is penance and when I do it then firstly in me the *Ākāśic* which means Space or Ether element will increase. I'll not go directly into *Paṛam Pṛakāś*. I cannot go. I have to go step-by-step."

"How does your *Ākāś Taṫva* or Ethereal element increase?" I inquired.

"It increases when I sit in meditation and one doesn't feel like speaking to anybody. You will not feel like eating anything as well. The more you have *Ākāś Taṫva* in you the people who are coming around you feel a special peacefulness. Their work will be done, their wishes will be granted, and peace will prevail. Your Godhood through the *Ākāś Tatva* will prevail upon them."

"But how do you increase the *Ākāś Tatva*?"

"The way we have told you…"

"To go beyond the beyond and meditate."

So basically this is what I understand. First fill yourself up with Light and recognize the Light Body within. Believe that you are the Spirit in the body and not the body. Keep focusing on this body of Light of yours within you. Then imagine your Light Body moving upwards, beyond the earth, beyond the Milky Way, beyond all the galaxies, upwards and upwards to the main source, and create your satellite or Light Body Image. It will help if you are doing this with sunlight streaming around or a beautiful glow of a candle or oil lamp. So now you are in front of the Great Flame. Then allow the Supreme Divine Radiance from the Great Flame to fill your Light body image and through that image of yours, let the Supreme Divine Light spread to all of creation by giving the right affirmations. I would recommend one to affirm to spread Oneness, Wellbeing, Love, Peace and Compassion to all, in all of Creation. And also imagine the Divine Light enter your body and charge your Light body and physical body. Then open your eyes and light a cigarette and exhale. The last part is not mandatory of course.

I focused back on to *Sakshi*.

"When your satellite image is up there, you feel that Divine Light with all its force entering your *Rūp* or Light Image and also entering your physical body. That Light which is entering your body is doing so through the universe and the cosmos. It is coming into your body. It is coming through your body. It is coming into your body through the image you have created, which is like your own personal satellite to gain that Light and Energy. The satellite which is you is an energy body. Firstly you have to create that. Once you create it, it is an instrument. Then you will spread it to others. So the more you get that Divine Light, that *Śakti* within you then only gradually your *Ākāś Taŧva* will increase. Then there are stages; there is the *Ākāś*, *Vāyu*, *Agni*, *Jal* and *Prithvi Taŧva*s. This comes gradually and step by step. So making a backward journey, you will first leave your *Dhàṛti Taŧva* or Earth element, then the element of Water, then Fire, then Air and finally the element of Vacuum or Space and then one becomes filled with Prime Elements."

"And if one keeps at it then one will go even beyond the Prime Elements and be filled *Paṛam Pṛakāś* or Supreme Divine Radiance which the Absolute Authority is made up of? Right?" I inquired and looked at *Bapuji.* He nodded with a twinkle in his eyes. He was like a small child listening to everybody, when the entire philosophy had come from him.

"By doing this meditation, one will be able to bring about change in all of creation and in the environment also. The more people meditate in this manner, giving the right affirmations, the better it is for all of creation. This is actually the technique of changing the whole cosmos. If you want to change it, it is very simple. Today if I go to a discotheque, I behave like the people in the discotheque. If I go to the temple, I behave in that manner. We are mainly influenced by the environment and atmosphere around us. If we change this atmosphere, this environment, automatically, the feelings and vibrations will change. So now what we are doing is changing ourselves. Also the same vibrations collectively are thrown on the globe, the cosmos and onto the entire creation. Then *Paṛam, Paṛam Sukh-Ṣanti;* Divine Joy and Peace will prevail. This Divine Joy and Peace will go to each and every soul, be it in the spirit form or any other form. In this way we also transform the whole world." *Sakshi* informed.

"Tell me one thing, do you feel mankind is ready for such philosophy or meditation or even change?" I asked *Sakshi*.

"No." She looked at all seated. *Anant* nodded too.

"So we are basically trying to slowly bring about a change in the mindset of all around; that each and every individual can basically contribute to the wellbeing of creation, apart from his or her own welfare? Isn't it?" I inquired. *Anant* began to speak.

"Mankind is not ready and that's why we always stick to 108 Primary Seed Souls or individuals. *Bapuji* has put forth such *Sañkalps* or intentions through his thoughts. Mankind is very attached to its mundane possessions and day-to-day survival and lifestyle. Very often the soul does not leave its *Sañskārs* or conditioning experiences even after death. It becomes, as you so often have quoted in *The Fakir* books, as earthbound. And because it holds onto those experiences, the soul remains earthbound and doesn't get liberated or move on."

"So what happens to somebody who isn't earthbound? What happens to an individual who has moved on? Where does he or she move on?" I asked.

"Just like *Bapuji* said that when one dies, they take their experiences, desires and beliefs with them and go on. So, you are a follower of *Sai Bābā* of *Shirdi*, so you will go to that part of the spirit world where all *Sai Bābā* of *Shirdi* followers reside. If I am a follower of *Jesus* and if I die and do not take birth again because I know that I'll come into the karmic cycle again and I have that knowledge and I'm that sensible to decide that I do not want to come again, then what I do is that according to my spiritual growth and the way I have been or spent my life physically as well as on the astral level – I sit there and I'll also make followers. I'll be sitting there and spreading the preaching of my Lord and Master."

"So what about life after death, what types of spirits exist and the various stages of spiritual growth and dimensions etc?"

"People say that we cannot go and live on Mars, reason being the elemental structure on Mars is different from that on Earth. Certain elements are missing and certain elements are present. If we change our body elements according to those elements suitable on Mars, then one can stay there and survive there. It is very simple. There are different astral levels too made of various elemental structures. They go about life the same way we go about ours but the only difference is here we have a five-elemental body, there they may have, three or two or one-elemental body. There is a book in *Gujarati*, *'Mrutyu Pachi Ni Duniya'* or *The World of Life After Death* written by *Aatmaram Patel*. There were two friends and one died. The dead friend's spirit or soul entered into his friend who was in search of God. He writes in the book that he was surprised to see that there is virtually the same world up there as it is down here. Yes, the only difference is that there the body is made of three elements and is very light and here the body is made of five elements. But beyond that virtually it is the same. Schools exist, temples, mosques, everything is there, but they have their own different composition of elements."

"Ok, fine, but I want to ask a very simple question. The author has given his reality of what's there… up there. He has given his reality. If a Christian were to die, as you said he would go to that part of the spirit world inhabited by Christians and I'm sure he might meet *Jesus*. If a Hindu were to die, he might meet Lord *Ram*, Lord *Šiva* or Lord *Kṛiṣna* or *Mā* depending upon his faith. Even *Mā's* appearance would depend on the belief you have held while on Earth. If you were a *Mā Duṛgā* worshipper I am sure you would meet *Mā Duṛgā* and if you are a *Mā Laxmi* worshipper, *Mā* would come in *Mā Laxmi's* form. If I were to die, I would meet *Bābā Sai* of *Shirdi*. But am sure that doesn't mean that *Bābā Sai* of *Shirdi* would come to everybody. He would come to me because of my love or *Bhav* that is there for Him. So, *Bābā Sai* is my reality, right or wrong?" I asked.

There was a unanimous vocal agreement from all present. *Anant* cleared his throat and spoke.

"What you have said is absolutely correct. If I pray to you, then I will only come to you and you will come for me. Even after you leave the body, I will pray to you, make your temples and always call out to you; you will then have to come to me."

"True *Anant*, but coming back to my question, *what is the real reality;* not yours, mine, jazzy *Laloo Prasad* with his designer underwear reality; but the Reality of all Realities; is there such a reality? What I'm trying to tell you is that, there are a few hundred thousand books on life in the spirit world. Books written by *Christians, Hindus, Buddhists, Zoroastrians, Native Americans,* and they all describe in detail life after death and the spirit world. You will never read of a Christian meeting Lord *Šiva,* the same way a Buddhist connecting to Lord *Christ* and a Native American interacting with Gods and Goddesses of other religions. But they all truly believe they have experienced life after death and been in the spirit world. Who is right? Who is wrong? Is there a reality beyond their reality? How does one unravel the reality beyond all illusions?" I inquired.

I also realized apart from all these realities, the Delhi cold had gotten into my bones and other parts of my anatomy in a real way.

"Nobody's wrong." *Sakshi* answered.

"The problem is that nobody is really right too!" I replied back.

Bapuji laughed aloud. He was enjoying this exchange.

"If you have read the *Śāstṛās*, they say that Lord *Viśnu* has made the world, some say that the world is made from the *Sañkalps* of Lord *Brāhṁā*, and sometimes they say that it's made from the *Sañkalps* of Lord *Śiva*. Maybe that is why it is written in the ancient texts that there are trillions of creations created every moment and destroyed every moment. If you have read our *Śāstṛās* – it is written that as there are millions of creations – it would automatically mean there are *koti-koti* or crores and crores of *Brāhṁā*, *Viśnu* and *Mahesh* too! Every world has its own God." *Anant* informed.

Soup arrived. *Bapuji* realized that I needed to be defrosted. It was cold and he gave me his thug cap to wear.

"Tell me about yourself *Bapuji*?"

"This is what I have heard." He began in *Gujarati*. "In my mother's body, a *Devi* would come, *Jogiṇi* – a very revered *Devi*, equivalent to *Mā Jagadamba*, they would say. There is a big temple of *Mā Jogiṇi*. She would come into my mother, tell her that tomorrow so-and-so thing is going to happen. Then she would tell us that Their *Rath* or chariot had come to take my mother's spirit away for sometime. That we should not be worried as my mother would come back into the body after a while. So what would happen is that my mother would become a dead body. They would take her spirit away and for two, sometimes for three days she would take a stroll in the spirit world and then be back into the body. Her body, as per medical science, would be considered a corpse. Thus, we would tell her to inform us well in advance when she would be leaving her body to roam the other side. Otherwise we'd take her for being really dead! From childhood, I would see different kinds of souls as I would work in the field. I was born in a very poor family. I am the son of a farmer. I have seen so much of poverty that you cannot imagine. We had *Chapals* or slippers to wear, no shoes, and wore clothes that were torn and in tatters. When I was in the fourth or fifth standard, I was a great *Bhakt* or devotee and disciple of *Bajarang Bali Hanumān*, and would keep a fast for Him. There was so much poverty around that I would speak to Him and pray to Him. I would sit in front of His idol at night when no one would be around. My prayer to Him was simple. I would tell Him: 'You give me so much power – as much as You had to lift the mountain – give me the energy Lord *Hanumān* and I will change the world because this world is not worth living. I will transform it and remove poverty.' I still feel great pain and am moved to tears when I see poverty and suffering. What is this world and life? Then I would sort of tell nasty things to God and say, 'Hey you the One Up there! Why did You create the world?'

"Those days I used to work in the fields even when I was a school kid – sometimes taking off from school to help in the fields. Those weren't easy days. Since childhood I had the *Sañkalp* that I would change the world and for that I began to read the *Gītā* from the fourth standard. But being still a child, I really could not understand the *Gītā*. In my school, my principal was a Brahmin who would preach the *Gītā*. And one day I barged into his chamber and argued with him. I asked him if God was formless or with form. I always believed that *Kṛiṣna* had a definite form, but He was a Messenger. He was Lord *Viśnu's Avatār*. So I would ask the Principal who was the energy behind *Kṛiṣna*. I wanted to know about the One who had the *Virāt Rūp* or the Majestic Form; the great image that reflects through the Messenger. I was verbally abused and told; 'You go to the field and do your farming as you are a farmer and will always remain a farmer! There is no food in your house, go work and stop getting into all this philosophy.'

"At the same time the *Gītā* preached that one should be a *Karmayogi,* meaning involved in meditative action and remain in the *Grahast Āśrăm* or living the life of a householder and all at once be spiritual and without attachment for results. The best of all *Aśhrăms* is the *Grahast Āśrăm.* The *Sanyāsa Āśrăm* – a phase when one goes in search of God leaving the family and responsibility of a householder living the life of an ascetic is not the greatest state or stage of spiritual life. Staying at home and being in the *Grahast Āśrăm* and still doing our duty; taking care of one's domestic responsibilities and family is the foremost and greatest duty. Taking care of our parents and family and yet being focused on God and spirituality is the best way of life. The *Gītā* says it like this: 'Living with the body and the body's relatives – yet being in the Image of the Soul – you have to forget all the body and bodily relationships to Remember Me.'

"Then after my tenth standard, I studied commerce in college and started to work with the Income Tax Department and funded my course in chartered accountancy, which I left half-way to complete my education in law. That's when I launched my own firm *Dashrath Patel & Co.* and took on cases of socially prominent people who were proved defaulters under law and under the penalty of the Income Tax department. While in service I used to raid the richest of the rich, some were innocent and some guilty, the one thing I realized was that nobody was truly happy and those same powerful and influential people would cry out and plead 'save me'. I had conducted many raids on the job. We were given a stipulated percentage of the amount raided but from the beginning I would never bring that money home. I just knew that ill-gotten cash can do nobody good. I have given lots of money to charity; lots of it to those in need.

"Then I realized that my heart, intellect and wisdom

were not interested in the workings of the material world and in the nights I would remember or recall that my true work was different. So I went off in search to many spiritual institutes and organizations and read most of the philosophical and religious books ranging from *Swāmi Vivekanand's* philosophy and literature, to the Quran, the Bible, the 18 *Veds*, 16 *Upanishads*, and 18 *Purāṇas.* I used to read them in my college days too. What came through was this: the *Ātmā* and the *Paṛam Ātmā* – the Individual Soul and the Cosmic Soul or Creator only really mattered; that the whole world is one big drama. So on one hand my search continued and self realization grew and on the other hand I was working in the most financially-centric world of Income Tax.

"But I realized that from the richest of the rich to the poorest of the poor, everybody was unhappy or just plain miserable. That is when I realized that only through Divine Wisdom can one really achieve happiness and liberation. My main philosophy is that in the world of the Infinite let *Paṛam, Paṛam, Paṛam* that is Supreme and Purest *Peace* and Joy prevail. I have started to impart these vibrations so that this *Paṛam, Paṛam, Paṛam Peace* and Happiness prevail in the world first. When the *Ātmā* falls into Karma *Bandhan* meaning bondage of destined Karma, only True Wisdom can free the soul from that bondage, nothing else can. You can do what you want but only through True Wisdom can you achieve liberation."

More soup arrived. Much needed. It was blasted cold. The *Paṛam Taṫva*s created by *Bapuji* I am certain could protect one from negative auras but Delhi winter like its politicians, was shameless; it entered the room anyway, entering my very bones and other parts of the anatomy I would rather not write about. Sipping the soup, I realized that what *Bapuji* said about wisdom was in a way true. Wisdom can get you to the doors of heaven but it is only selfless love for one and all, true compassion for one and all and your Master's grace that is going to get you into the realm of Oneness. But I guess when you get truly wise, not spiritually intellectual but truly wise, then selfless love and true compassion are bound to come about and the Grace of the Master has to be present. As without the Grace of the Master, how can one get truly wise? Back to *Bapuji*.

"Why did the soul come into Karma *Bandhan* or karmic bondage… mainly due to *kṛodh* or anger, *moh* or desire and attachments and *Ahañkār* or pride. So the soul gets entangled and cries and screams for release. What do we do then? We connect the person with his or her own *Paṛam Ātmà Swarūp* that is the Divine Supreme Soul Image of One's Self, his or her own *Paṛam* or Supreme Image. *Betā*, you have one serious issue with yourself?" *Bapuji* pointed towards me as I was sipping on piping-hot soup and took a fool-hardy large-gulp that sort-of burnt one of those necessary pipes in the throat. "The problem with you is that you don't want to believe who you are? You keep undermining yourself? I don't like that about you."

I wanted to disagree. I didn't undermine myself. I didn't need to. I had a large section of the populace who undermined me vociferously on a religiously regular basis.

"Anyway there are also the *Paṛam Ātmās* which means those *Pavitra Ātmās* or pure souls that have the capability of transforming the world. And why have they taken birth… to transform this world. Their *Ātmā* has so much power, if only they believe in themselves and the Oneness of creation. If they believe: 'I am soul-conscious and that my duty is to make everybody soul conscious, give knowledge and transform the world. And transform it soon.'

"It is no more feasible to stay on this earth. Natural calamities have increased – all five elements are imbalanced. And the only way is to go first with prayer and thought to the Source; make your Image and then transform the world. Can you imagine if the original 108 were to realize themselves, then the nine-lakh souls will follow immediately in a second. Some of the 108 Souls are in the spirit and some are in the body. The *Ākāri Ātmās* or spirit-forms are very, very powerful. They will catch hold of the *Sākāri* or the physical-forms and bring them down to us. They will be the super most souls… they would be super souls by now, super *Ātmā*. So the spirit bodies will bring the physical of the 108 Souls together. There are super *Ātmās*, some from the group of 108, some from the group of sixteen thousand, some from the nine lakh; there are many super-souls here on planet earth. And in the *Ākāri* image… when we give them a call they start moving around you. Yesterday when you came here, there were so many souls with you."

I nearly poured the soup all over me. For a while *Bapuji* spoke to me about myself and we shall for obvious reasons keep that out of this book. Stuff that made sense and some stuff that if I were to publish, my good readers would think *Bapuji* and I were smoking some very debatable herbs, while he revealed what he did.

"As we keep meditating and becoming one with the Light, slowly we regain our spiritual power and then we can help all those associated with us. Nearly all of creation is in pain. They scream in their hearts and are praying for peace. The Seed Souls have to respond. Once the soul will be *enlightened*, then the body will lighten up. The *Sūkśṃ* or subtle body will glow. When the individual is tensed, the subtle body gets discharged. This discharge of the subtle body affects the gross body. Remember we are what we eat and what we think. Because in our food is the body. When we breathe air, air is the body. Our body is made of five elements but now the food that we eat and the air we breathe is filled with negativity. You take in air, in the air, there's negative energy. The *Vāyu Mandàḷ* is filled with negativity. *Vāyu* also means thoughts. So, if the *Vāyu* is filled with negativity the air we breathe too is completely filled with negativity as thoughts travel through the air. So even if someone wants to perform positive Karma, he or she cannot do so even if the person is by heart a pure soul. There are a lot of people who wish from within to do good for the world and have a desire to uplift creation. The foremost souls are loaded with pure and noble intent; their *Rooh* or their souls only have positive, world enhancing desires. They want good for one and all and work for the betterment of the world. Work without any expectations. And if anybody works without any expectations, that person's *Bhāgya* or destiny and future shines forth. *Niśkām* or selfless Karma without any *Bhāvnā* or intent; not even considering karmic salvation; that person slowly becomes God like."

This is true. Often in channelling *Bābā Sai* has said that however good our actions may be, but if there is any give and take in our intentions, if one is seeking something, even karmic gain or cleansing, then the person in a strange way is getting further entangled in Karma. The path of Light is paved with subtle dark alleys. Be careful. I once again focused on *Bapuji*.

"When the work is done with a *Nishkām* attitude, for example, just do work or serve selflessly then that is *Nishkām* Karma. The philosophy of Karma says one thing, when we all do work to spread light and happiness, then one is moving towards God and becoming one with the Light. Or else one is caught up with the give and take of Karma. And the sad part is however pure a soul may be, even if a Master in previous life, were to come into the body, there is a chance even the Master might get sucked into this karmic play. Once in the body we are caught up with five elements and from soul conscious, all of us become body conscious. What happens with being body conscious is that the attachment with the body and relationships of the body come in the way. Then, there is the question of livelihood; survival. Why is more than half of the world unhappy? What is the reason for universal sadness? The root cause is desires and more desires and then more desires. Nothing is enough. Wants, expectations, desires, just never ends. I want I want I want… it just never ends. You have been told the same haven't you *Ruzbeh*?"

I nodded. It's true isn't it? When you look around, what is that we need for our real happiness? Not comfort and wants, but for genuine happiness; nothing external is needed. Pure happiness is a state of centeredness, a state of calmness that comes through with complete positive surrender. Happy and joyous surrender is all that's needed. Think of the times you were happy and in peace... and you will realize that more often than not, the sense of centeredness and happiness came from within and not outside and it didn't cost a dime or one's sanity to experience that state of calmness and happiness. Basic comfort and good health and one's sense of wellbeing is very important but to spend one's entire lifetime in the pursuit to acquire and accumulate more and more is an exercise in futility and a walk through a large track of sinking sand. We all know that the only thing we take with us when we leave the body for good, is one's Karma and still all our lives we are focused on everything but the true wealth of Oneness. I focused on *Bapuji* again.

"What is really needed? A clean and simple lifestyle; a few clothes, clean bed, nourishing food; loved ones; but in reality true happiness comes from within… our very within. But aren't we all running after more cars, better phones, expensive jewellery, false sense of honour and respect, but does all this give true happiness; that is a question each one has to ask? I have seen much of the world... just imagine, I have conducted more than three hundred income tax raids, so what would I have not seen? In front of us people would suffer and even die of shock or fear. I have myself admitted people to the hospital; rich influential people who were scared and were suffering; why because of their pursuit of that extra crore or large piece of jewellery. So after seeing this type of life and seeing how fragile the richest and the most influential known people in society were, those who outwardly have it all, sadness filled me up. I wanted to do something for the world. Change it. The voice from within would say... this world cannot go on... But I didn't know how to go about it or do something constructive about it. Because the *Vidhi* or procedure I did not know.

"In India there are 25,000 *Sampradās* or townships. And in a village also when someone who has done some good work dies they make his statue and after a while they begin to worship him and also there is the Village God or Goddess, or *Grām Dev* or *Devi.* Each village will have a separate God or Goddess. They are souls that protect the village but to the ability of Their spiritual power. All over the country we have so many *Śrī Ram* temples. And then there was Babar who broke into the *Ram Mandir.* My question even as a child was that if Babar raided the main temple of *Śrī Ram*, how come *Śrī Ram* didn't make the invader blind or stop the invader from looting His own temple. The *Swaminārāyan Mandir* had terrorism activity a few years back; bullets were fired and people killed in its premises in *Gandhinagar*. Many of those who come to me, who were from the *Swaminārāyan* sect, came to me and asked me why did such an act take place? I asked them only one question. Where is your God? If people are not safe even in Temples and Mosques and *Gurudwaras* and Churches and bullets are fired and devotees are killed in a place of worship then where is your God?

"Most of the 33-crore Goddesses and Gods, Prophets,

Planetary Gods, most of them are now in the physical body, sucked into the karmic wheel and cesspool of give and take; some are still in the spirit world but in the three-elemental *Ākāri Rūp* and in that form even They are powerless. Their three-elemental subtle body is made of *Vāyu or* Air, *Agni* that's Fire and *Ākāś* or Space. In that if the element of *Vāyu* is poisonous or filled with negativity it will give rise to *Rāg-Dwesh* or Anger and Rage and further corrupt the other elements. The three-elemental spirits who are possessed with anger and rage and lust also enter into people and get all wrong work done through them. So even those who once were most powerful have in some way lost their power and become weak. They too want freedom from the hold of negative elements, Karma and bondage. And true freedom can only come through when one's entire focus is on The Creator and going back to the Source. Whether a person is from the 108 Souls or sixteen-thousand or nine-lakhs and so on, the fact is each one needs to go back to his or her source. Remember from the Absolute Authority, came the Supreme Father of the Infinite, from whom came 108 Souls and then sixteen-thousand, then nine-lakh, then two-crore, and then six-and-half-crore, then thirteen-crore, then thirty-three-crore and it went on and on… then there were *Anant Koti Brähṁāñḍs* or the endless-crore galaxies… *Arabo and Kharabo Brähṁāñḍs* that is trillions and hundreds-of-billion galaxies created. Infinite creations were made. All this led to a general loss of power in their Creators. So, only when you call out to the main Power House will things start to change. But each one can do his or her bit by going to the Source. I believe that when the 108 and all those who came through them, consciously or subconsciously begin to focus on the Absolute Authority and visualize and meditate on merging with that Authority, things will start to change. Imagine all of us meditating and with intent calling down upon divine vibrations of peace and wellbeing? Tell me son, won't things get better then? This will collectively awaken one and all, give you your sense of duty, remind you of your duty... keep visualizing all life forms to awaken to their original form... awaken, awaken, awaken... awaken. Take your family, that is, your extended family. In your family there will be super souls.... gradually you will have the 'power of experience'. Whichever soul comes in front of you, you will gradually have the power to decipher, discriminate, grow to understand which category it fits in; whether *Viśwa Kalyānkāri,* proactive in world welfare or progress, *Viśwa Parivartak* or helpful in changing or if it is *Viśwa Seva Dhāri,* service oriented. They want to serve the world, why? Because there is a *Mālik,* there is a Creator, and all creations are the children of the Creator.

"Your children are shouting. When your children are shouting, then their vibrations and grief will touch you, right? As you make your satellite more powerful you will be able to help you lot. Your creation will gain power and if they want *Mokśa* then they will become your cell and come back to your subtle body. That's when you will have more power. That's when you will go back to the *Divya* or Divine World. Till the time they scream in pain, your creation whichever cell of yours it has emanated from... that cell will disturb you... it will create restlessness within you; depression; you will wonder why am I so restless and depressed but the true reason is that those who belong to you are miserable and their misery is reaching you."

6

At night *Meher* and I strolled about in the garden of the hotel. It was among the city's best resorts and had some wonderful open spaces. *Meher* and I had just seen a few cartoons where the Gods – Lord *Brähmā and Śivji* were granting boons to demons. With as profound body-structures as theirs, the demons didn't look like they were losing much sleep over their cholesterol content! Once boons were granted by the Gods to these demons, the latter went about giving the same Gods the mother of all migraines.

"What I don't understand is that when the Gods know that these demons are going to *doos* bad things, They still go about granting them whatever is asked. Is that right Daddy?"

"Sometimes the Gods can be as nuts as us love."

"I wouldn't just go about giving gifts to these demons. First of all they don't dress up well. Secondly they are demons."

"I know love. Gods are too liberal with their gifts."

"Did you get my gift which I asked for Daddy?"

Ahhhh… This was now going to be tricky. I had an inkling as to why Gods were so liberal granting gifts – to appease the demons who or else would start throwing a mother of all tantrums.

"Did you get that Barbie who can sing?"

I know very well what to do with whoever created Barbie and it is rather unprintable.

"Uh...ahh...I forgot love."

My daughter started to snort. Like a bull in the arena, never a good sign for any parent.

"Gods are granting gifts to demons and you aren't getting me my gifts."

"You technically aren't a demon my love though one could debate about this."

"You are calling me a *demons* now, I hate you Daddy. You are a demon."

"Yes my love have been called a demon many times before."

"I didn't mean to say you are those demons. You are just another demon."

"Let's go and watch more cartoons about what the Gods are up to."

"These Gods are also demons. You are also a demon and this Delhi cold is horrible."

Next morning I was back in the *Āśrăm* and was seated in the Meditation Hall with *Mataji, Anant* and *Sakshi*.

"As written in the *Gītā,* the Wise One has many *Avatārs*. What does *Avatār* mean? *Avatār* means those who are *Nyārā* from *Janam* and *Maran* or beyond the cycle of birth and death," informed *Mataji*. "It is said that if an *Avatār* touches anything with intent then that turns into gold. What is that energy that can with intent turn dust into gold? In reality what it means is that an *Avatār* is the One who when touches our *Buđhi* or intellect, can convert ignorance into wisdom, which means God consciousness. So what is that energy? Where does that energy come from? An *Avatār* is said to have thirty-two qualities or *Guṇās,* one of which is that of the Alchemist. The power of being an Alchemist comes from the Absolute Authority; call Him or Her by whatever name you want to; but the ability to convert darkness into

Light can come only from the Primordial Creator, and it's then passed forth down.

"What is *Avatāran betā*? As it is told in the *Gītā*, 'O *Arjun*, *Avatāran* happens to me, and I do not go into the mother's womb'. Similarly, let us reflect on the Divine Body that we have in the form of Light. The Divine Body of Light that we have is weightless. So, our Light body is similar to the body we have on earth."

Ok now my two bit. Now you may wonder how come that Spirit body is in the image of the physical body of this incarnation, as obviously we have had countless bodies through our innumerable reincarnations. So either our Spirit body only reflects our physical body of that present incarnation or then logically we should have various Spirit bodies floating around in the cosmos. I believe that the lifetime in which we become one with the Light, that lifetime is the one we have truly lived and thus the image of that particular lifetime becomes all important and the Light Body will resemble the body of that lifetime where soul realization takes place. Of course this is my rock-and-roll spiritualism. Back to *Mataji*.

"Just as we were once only Prime Light our world was also Prime Radiance. Then we became spirits and our world also became three elemental. When we became physical, the world also became five elemental. Just as the seed is, the tree will be the same. So if you now want to transform the world, you will have to catch the seed, The Creator only… nothing else will do! We want the main seed. How will we find the seed? So in the *Gītā*, this too is elaborated upon: 'O *Arjun*, This is an upturned tree. When the tree rots… when the tree completely turns into tatters… when it becomes old; that's when I come into the seed form.' When the tree rots completely the seed comes up. The seed can never be destroyed. The seed remains. In the same way when creation is destroyed, the Creator remains. When the elements are filled with negativity and all seems to be lost, He will infuse the elements with His Energy and Breath and a new life will come about. Amidst the many storms, it is only the Divine Image that is awake. Through relinquishing the body's relationships with the outside world and in becoming the image of the soul, in remembrance of the *Paṛam Ātmā,* that's when all sins will be destroyed. How will it be? It is something to ponder about.

"For me, it works in a simple way. When our Light body will be awakened and we will remember it in our Master's Light body; I will remember *Bapuji's* Light body, you will remember it in *Sai Bābā* of *Shirdi's* Light body or the Body of Radiance, and when we immerse ourselves in our Master's Radiant body, all our Karmas through the fire of *Yog* will be destroyed within a second; similar to, as we put anything into the fire and do a *Swāhā* and it becomes an offering. Similarly, in our *Yog Agni,* whatever Karmas are present they will be destroyed or annihilated. All our sins will be nullified."

We then walked up to *Bapuji's* room and entered within. He stood up and gave me a warm embrace, made sure I had a blanket covering my body, as it was terribly chilly.

"How many civilizations like ours exist? How many similar five-elemental civilizations are there in all?" I inquired. *Mataji* immediately replied.

"There is only one world of five elements and that's our planet Earth. There are no five-elemental worlds anywhere else. There are worlds with four elements, with two elements, even one-elemental, but five-elemental bodies are only on planet earth. That is why we call Her, Mother Earth. That is why ancient scriptures say that even the *Devatās* or Demi Gods are not fortunate enough to have been born as humans. They say that human birth is the only fortunate incident as it is only in the form of humans that we can achieve and attain *Paṛam Ātmā* or Godhood or the Supreme Soul. However evolved a soul may be, till the soul has not worn the garb of a human body, it can never achieve Godhood. The way to live is to transform the world, get it on a progressive path, do positive and noble work for all, and all will eventually merge in peace and happiness with the One they have emerged from. That is why we have to do *Yog*. Let *Bapuji* explain to you further."

"Son," *Bapuji* spoke to me in *Gujarati*. "In this world, the main reason for unhappiness and disquietude is that we are caught up in things which are finite and ignoring things which are infinite. Do you understand what I mean by finite and the infinite? Finite means desires, wishes or wants. Now where do desires, wishes and wants come from? They come from looking at each other.

"Why has the world turned-out to be like this? Earlier the world was *Satva Pradhān* or ruled by pure truth. It was Absolutely True. It was *Paṛam Satya* or of the highest supreme truth. From *Paṛam Satya* we have reached *Tamo Pradhān*. *Satva, Rajas* and *Tamas* are three basic *Vrutis* or natural dispositions or characteristics of everything in the world. The same soul that was *Paṛam, Paṛam, Paṛam Ātmā,* has descended to the level of what we see in the world today. That same purest of the purest of the pure soul became subjected to various forms of distractions and environments. From *Paṛam Ātmā* it became just *Ātmā*. Why did our soul fall from Grace? Why did we come from the purest of the pure elements to be caught up with earthly five elements? This is the *Sthool* or the gross or the physical world; *Loukik* or tangible or substantial also called corporal or material world. In this world desires, wants, wishes are the foundations for unhappiness and disquietude. So, where did the desires and wants arise from… they arose when we began looking at each other and comparing or wanting what the other had.

"That's why today a person may not have the capacity to own a cycle, but wants a two-wheeler. A person may not have the capacity for a two-wheeler, but desires a car. One can barely maintain one small car but wants a big fancy car. So you start taking loans and then repaying the loans becomes a weight around your neck, so frustrations and sadness arises. Then, there are wants of physical relations and relationships. Those desires begin to entrap the individual and then the soul weeps. One begins to get caught-up more in the five elements and karmic bondage.

"When you have knowledge and apply it, you are set free. We get our bodies and relatives and physical relationships as per the tally and accounts of our Karmas and once the Karmas are exhausted, the relationships drop off. But the soul is *Amar Avināśi*; forever and indestructible. The soul cannot be destroyed. As Karmas began to come about, the soul got tied-up with karmic calculations, tally of the Karmas, etc. When someone leaves the body, depending on the Karmas and the wisdom of the individual, the soul either occupies another body or resides in the spirit world. The soul is made of intellect and desires, apart from individuality. Whatever is there isn't only the intellect but also desires. Let us assume the individual is in the spirit plane but has desires of the body and is attached to relatives and relationships still in the physical plane; thus, the soul becomes earth-bound and sort-of hovers around loved ones or things it is still attached to.

"There are various subtle or astral worlds. Gravity on the earth's surface is up to 200 kilometres and it holds three-elemental spirits. We call them ghosts but they are ordinary people who are in the spirit body still attached to the world and gross objects. Of these, maybe a small percentage of spirits want to carryout positive work but to get the good work done, they need a medium. Only a human can be a medium. They cannot enter an animal and speak through them. Unless one is like *Sant Jñāneśwar* who made a buffalo recite the *Vedās*. But He is a Master Supreme.

"So all those positive *Ātmās* or spirits look-out for the support of positive mediums who can become instruments or vessels to spread goodness and light. Many times they do not get such a person or sometimes they may get a human being who is filled with negativity also. But even when a positive medium is found, they have to send positive rays into the deep subconscious mind of the medium, and then into the unconscious mind and then connect the unconscious to the subconscious and get work done through the conscious mind. It's a beautiful process. It's a very deep concept. Intellect and experiences are part of our soul journey. Where does the soul reside? It resides in our *Anjanā or Ājñā Chakra,* also known as the Third Eye *Chakra*, and the centre point of this *Chakra* is the soul's abode.

"Now where did desires come from in the soul? The soul is *Amar Avināśi* or forever and immortal; and first when it was born, the soul was without desire and selfless; it had power, it had *Paṛam Pṛakāś*, that's Supreme Divine Radiance or Divine *Light*, so it was *Paṛam Ātmā*. Then the *Paṛam Ātmā* created the *Dev Ātmās* or Demi Gods and the *Divya Ātmās* or Divine Souls. The *Divya Ātmās* were living in the divine state and had divine bodies. From the *Divya Lok* we came down to the various celestial levels. That's when innumerable worlds were created and then the *Sūkśṃ Vatan* or the Astral Worlds were created and *Anant Koti Brāhṁāñḍs* or countless crore galaxies were created. Each creation had a separate *Devatā*; the *Devatā* of this *Brāhṁāñḍ* was *Indra.* And eventually as our Scriptures teach us, even *Indra* – the King of Demi Gods became a worm in hell. So imagine even the astral God became a worm in hell. Imagine the ramification of desires, pride, moving away from knowledge and wisdom and the Light, that even the King of all Demi Gods too became a worm in hell."

I pondered over this. I would have preferred to ponder over this statement smoking a cigarette but that being out of question I spiritually put a pencil in my mouth and pondered. Imagine the power of thoughts and desires that they can make even the Gods go nuts? What about us poor imbecile human beings. No wonder we are so professionally roggered and messed up. Back to *Bapuji.*

"*Indra's* Karmas were such that He had to pay for his actions and there are no exceptions where karmic rules are concerned. If you read *Indra's* story, you will realize that He had committed very heavy Karmas. He was cursed by *Gautam Ruśi* due to His behaviour towards the *Ruśi's* wife. That's when *Indra* was cursed. So, when desires and attachments blind you, illusions bring even the Gods down and there are no exceptions."

So, in short, most of us are going to meet each other in the bowels of hell, I mused. Great!

"The only escape from attachment and illusions is knowledge and through knowledge and application of knowledge one goes into *Vairāgya* or detachment. Who are your biggest enemies? What has the *Gītā* said? Your biggest enemies are your 'body and your body's relations'. They make you cry. Who makes you cry? Not strangers. Your loved ones make you cry. And why did the body and through the body, relationships and one's family and friends come about? Because of the karmic give and take. Now how did the Karma *Bandhan* or karmic give and take come about? Through attachments and desires and that is through lack of knowledge and being attached to the world and its outcome. Now the only way out from this karmic entanglement is through detachment and that detachment will come through knowledge and wisdom. You have to cut-off the Karma *Bandhan* or karmic entanglement."

Here I need to add my two bit. I don't believe it's just knowledge that is going to free one-and-all from karmic entanglement. We all know what's wrong and right and what's good for our spiritual growth and what's not. We have the knowledge but yet we keep screwing up. Keep messing up our karmic balance sheet. It's not just knowledge; it's the right use of our Free Will and unwavering Priority to serve The Light and the need to make our Master happy and proud of us which is going to make us move onwards spiritually. When all these three forces combine and move in the same direction, then and only then, I feel one starts getting free from karmic entanglement. But then this is my logic. Anyway back to *Bapuji*.

"Now one thing I will tell you. The soul needs peace and happiness. What kind? It needs *Paṛam* or Supreme Joy and Peace. And that is also the right of the soul. The soul is *Śāñtrūp* or in the Image of Silence. The soul is Silence. It requires peace and requires *Paṛam Ākāś Tatva* or the Pure Element of Ether. So where did desires inside the *Ātmā* come from? The *Ātmā* was desireless in the *Paṛam Dhām*, so then where did the *Sañkalps* or desires come from? *Sañkalps* initially were very subtle but even subtle desires are desires nonetheless. So where did the desires come from? From the mind or intellect and that is why we say be careful what you say or do or think, as they create their own ramifications and their own worlds. As the *Ātmā* starts to fall, due to desires… it starts to look at others – what you see is what you will think. So when you think – with the *Sañkalps* you create vibrations. Your subtle aura changes to various vibrations that come about from thoughts and desires– when you think negative, that's when your subtle body becomes black. There's a computer programme where you can see your aura. They captured your *Mataji's* aura..."

"Yes I was there. The aura was snow white." *Anant* informed. *Bapuji* continued.

"Why was her aura pristine white? When is the aura white? When there is calmness or *Śāñti* and only peace resides; when you are in the image of your soul and you have the knowledge of your soul the aura is pure white. So being in the image of the *Ātmā*, the complete subtle body, inside our gross body, becomes pure and then the gross body follows with purity too. Inside our gross body there is a subtle body. So, by being *Nih-Sañkalp* and being still in *Jñān* or wisdom, and being in the image of the soul, we can realize that the soul is *Nih-Sañkalp*. That's called *Jñān Jal*. They say that, 'the Water becomes calm', in our body, and two third of our body is water and if the water within is calm we are calm too. So by gaining our *Jñān Jal*, we will become *Shānt* or peaceful. That's when the *Jal Tatva* or water element exerts its power. By being in peace, the subtle aura becomes white, pure white.

"If you think creative and positive thoughts and thoughts for the benefit and progress of the world, your aura or your subtle body will be blue in colour; so blue colour represents creativity. When you are angry, the aura will be black or red. Mostly it is red. And when one thinks negative, absolutely negative thoughts then the aura turns black. Yellow is also a very positive colour; while the colour purple is also called the golden colour!"

Ok, I need to validate this machine that checks the aura. The machine that *Bapuji* spoke about is actually a software programme created by Harry Oldfield. When I was editing a magazine for *Indian Express* called *Holistic Healing*, I was invited by a doctor who had a small clinic in *Santacruz*, in *Mumbai*. Those days I was also the Consulting

Editor to another publishing house run by *Sunit Banerjee*, a dear friend now. So when I got a call from this doctor – whose name for-the-life-of-me I cannot recollect – and he requested me to come over and see the new software programme that recorded auras. I agreed for the simple reason that the clinic was a five-minute-walk from *Sunit's* office.

One afternoon I entered this doctor's clinic. It was either on the first or the second floor. It was a simple one-room clinic with a table and a few chairs on the right. There was a computer on the table and wires that connected to a handy cam. Those days' electronic items were large instruments. If you had a handy-cam and a mobile phone then, you could go to war with any of the many neighbouring countries with a very secure state of mind. They were not the present-day pansy, small, compact, state-of-the-art hardware. The mobile phone was heavy enough and large enough to fight-off at least ten muscular women. Anyway, at the farthest side of the room, there was a white bed sheet hung-up, and in front of the sheet was a plastic chair which was a few feet away, in front of the handy-cam.

"I called you here as I needed to show you how this software works." Spoke the doctor whose name I still can't remember. He made me sit on the chair in front of the camera and behind was the white bed sheet and he switched on the camera and after a while he shut it off.

"Come and have a look."

So I approached the computer and saw a very blurred image of myself with colours swirling round me.

"This programme records the aura of an individual. It's actually meant for medical purposes, as illnesses first show on the aura of the individual and then seep into the body." The doctor informed. This is true. Earlier days, Sufis and Masters would carry peacock feathers and when you approached the Master, He would sort-off whirl the peacock feathers above your head and around your body. In reality, He was clearing and cleaning your aura. The Master could see your aura clearly and He would recognize which part of your body was getting affected by an incoming disease or if you were already ill, then by cleaning your aura one could either get cured or the hold of the illness would reduce substantially. Of course, even now there are folks who go about with peacock feathers and they don't caress you with it but sort-of, thrash you about. They can't see the aura but when you go to *Sufi Darghas*, the caretaker will first touch the feathers to the Master's Shrine, and then caress your head, around your body, and pat your back with it. Even though the caretaker has no vision to see auras, the fact that the feathers have touched the Master's Shrine, does wonders.

Anyway the doctor told me a lot of complimentary things about me and my aura and I thought he was nuts. My first book on the paranormal, *The Last Marathon* had recently been published and thus a lot of what he told me could have come from inference and not so much from the aura software. As the editor of the magazine I was the one who would finally decide whether one of my team members would interview him and then approve the article to be published; so putting me up a coconut tree made sense for the doctor.

"Why don't you get somebody I would never have heard of and then if the aura reading is accurate, you can also believe all that I have told about yourself and the authenticity of this software."

So we agreed and fixed a day and time and two weeks later I took a family friend, an elderly man, like an uncle, let us call him *Mr. K.*, to the doctor, whose name I still can't remember. I can remember the uncle's name but not the doctor's; am just clarifying in case you jump to conclusions.

All through the journey *K.* kept talking about how

his wife was driving him not up the wall but through the blasted wall. *K.* was about sixty-odd years old then, but he was in very good physical shape. He was an ardent yogi, who did yoga every day and meditated since he was a young boy. He prayed the *Avesta* prayers for hours every day and went to the Fire Temple often. *Avesta* is the sacred text of us *Zoroastrians*. He helped the poor and was very generous to the needy and the ailing. His Waterloo was his relationship with his wife. They individually were good souls but as husband and wife, were like two peas in a septic tank. So for an hour *K.* spoke of nothing but his wife. Like most devoted husbands, he didn't speak anything complimentary.

We arrived and *K.* was asked to sit on the chair and our doctor began to go about like *Satyajit Ray*, shooting a movie. I sat and looked at the screen. I could see the usual colours, predominantly green but with a thin layering of black. The doctor switched off the camera and then focussed his attention on the computer screen and began to talk.

"He is a very generous man. Prays a lot and really helps those in need. The colour green signifies that. But do you see that thin black layer. Well that is not his permanent aura colour but obviously he has had a fight with somebody and holds immense anger towards that person." Without batting an eyelid the doctor turned towards *K.* "Are you married, sir?" Like a man confessing to a major crime, *K.* nodded sheepishly. "Ahhhhh, in all probability this anger is towards his wife, who he has had a long association of....uhhhh...uhhhhh...."

"We get it doc. He is married. That says it all." I chipped in with my phenomenal wisdom.

"Yes. You don't get along with your wife. There's too much pent-up frustration as-well-as expressed anger. Am I right sir?"

K. nodded again. The doctor then spoke for another five minutes and I had to agree that the software worked. I looked at *K.*

"Will you shut your eyes and begin to pray. I want to see if anything happens to your aura."

K. nodded. For two minutes his eyes remained shut and then he began to chant *Aum*. For the first two minutes when he had shut his eyes, praying inwardly, the black coating around his principal aura covering began to dim, and then when he began to chant *Aum* loudly, the black coating slowly disappeared and then the green colour became more enhanced and other beautiful colours began to come about.

"Ok now think of your wife." I spoke aloud. *K.* immediately opened his eyes. "Think of what happened in the morning and the fight, uncle *K.*"

He shut his eyes and within a few seconds the black coating began to cover his aura. What prayers and God could achieve in two minutes, the wife negated it in a few seconds. I tell you the power of women is astounding.

Anyway back to *Bapuji.*

"But where did the colours originate from? Absolute Authority is present in the form of Supreme Light, the Supreme Divine Radiance or *Paṛam Pṛakāś*. From this Supreme Divine Radiance came the Founding Father of the Infinite and through Him came the 108 *Paṛam Ātmās* or the Supreme Souls. The *Paṛam Ātmās* had nothing in them, not even colour. Then the *Paṛam Taŧvas* or pure elements came about. Through *Sañkalps* or thoughts, intentions and pledges, the whole of creation was made. Whatever you see today, the fruits and the flowers and everything around is created with somebody's *Sañkalps* or intentions. If you notice, when you think too hard or desire too intensely, you will feel your energy depleted. That is because thoughts or desires create a deficiency in the subtle body. By using your thought power, you will notice there will be a deficit of energy. If your mind is perpetually occupied with varied thoughts etc. you will find a deficit in the soul's power. Then you notice a deficit in the *Paṛam Taŧvas*. That's when the heaviness sets in.

"Just like… let's take *Vāyu Taŧva* or the Wind element; there is negativity in the *Vāyu Taŧva*. If a spirit soul is in a negative state, it means that the element of *Vāyu* within the spirit or ghost is poisonous. The pure spirit that is positive will have *Pṙāṇa* as *Vāyu Taŧva*. And in that Wind element the element of Fire too is present and that is how smoke is created. Often you will see a spirit look hazy or as though covered with smoke. So many-a-times a spirit looks like a cloud of smoke or just looks hazy white and even though the spirit may want to show itself to you, it may not have the power to manifest itself, and you too may not have the power to see it. Why is it that we can't see spirits as clearly as we see everything else in the world? That is because we are made of five elements while the spirit is made of three elements. If you want to see a ghost who is comprised of three elements, then you have to become of three elements too."

"But there are many psychics who can see spirits but they aren't made up of three elements?" I inquired and I also mused, pondered and contemplated, that I knew a number of psychos… sorry… psychics, who could be three-elemental as they don't resemble or behave like human beings at all.

"You can see three-elemental spirits through *Divya Druśti* my son, through meditation one gets *Ātmā Jñān* or soul knowledge and then *Divya Druśti* or divine vision is acquired. You can see anything with *Divya Druśti*. But for that, we have to do *Yog*."

"What *Yog* is that?"

"I'll tell you. For *Yog* there is a need for an atmosphere

or a *Vāyu Mandàḷ*. Like for example, in this room I have increased the amount of *Paṛam Taṭva or* Prime Elements. Now, if I want someone to experience a particular paranormal occurrence, I will call only that one person in this room. If another person is sitting in this room, and let us assume that person's astral body is black in colour or filled with anger or hate or jealousy, I will be unable to make you experience anything. That's why some of the great yogis lived in caves. They didn't want anything. If I get into *Yog*, I do not bathe for days and do not change my clothes for days. I do not change clothes for even a month but from my body you will get a lovely fragrance. My clothes too have my aura residue. Also, I do not allow just anybody to cook for me or even wash my clothes. Why? The food that I eat if not cooked by somebody with the right aura is going to affect my body and through my body my aura too. Even if my clothes are washed by somebody not in the same wavelength, once I wear those clothes, their negativity is bound to affect me. It is a very subtle thing. I do not allow any and everybody to meet me now. Earlier I used to meet one-and-all but I realized that the other person's rubbish gets transferred to me. Their wants and illnesses cling to my aura and then pass on to my body. I am suffering from blood pressure and diabetes. I never had it before and there was no reason for illnesses like blood pressure and rise in sugar levels in my body. Nobody in the family has got these issues then why me? Those who come in front of me, all their diseases get transferred into me."

I shifted with unease. I have more illnesses than fleas on my neighbour's neurotic, high-strung dog. My heart went out to *Bapuji*.

"So then I gradually stopped meeting people. I experienced a lot; that when we are in the image of light or in the subtle form – the auras of others, which are negative can play havoc with one's state of health; so I slowly went into seclusion. This room is filled with *Paṛam Taŧva* or prime elements created by my intentions. If I allow anyone negative to come in and if that person's subtle body is slightly negative and as a result the subtle body is discharged obviously the space will be filled with black aura. The person's subtle body will be negative. That will not allow me to listen to your knowledge and not allow you to listen to mine and in between us there will be a hindrance in the exchange of knowledge. Now, only when the One above gives clear direction, only then I meet the person, otherwise I do not meet. For you also I got clear direction that I must meet you and that through you a great work is destined to take place. The direction comes clear from up. First, one needs to give complete knowledge, let the person drown into the ocean of knowledge and then make him experience the gained knowledge. I was told clearly that till the time you don't experience the knowledge, how would you write about it? Now the person who will write the book needs to know and experience everything and only then that individual can talk or write about this divine truth."

There was a knock and *Sakshi* entered the room. There was some talk and I pondered about 'transference and mingling of auras'. The fact is we don't have the inclination or the environment, where we can seclude oneself from the world. We go about into the world for various reasons. Thus, to make sure negativity in the aura or intentions does not latch on to our aura, it is mandatory to meditate or say prayers of protection as often as you can. It could be a half-a-minute prayer of protection or some chant that goes on in your mind. It's a must. There is no other way to safeguard one self. Pray to the Sun or the flame for cleansing and protecting your aura. Touch your forehead to the ground in gratitude and surrender to Mother Earth. These little gestures of surrender and prayers will protect you and your lot. And of course keep chanting your Master's name. That is one's shield against all negativity from the outside world; burning away of the karmic baggage from one's aura and giving one protection against one's own stupidity too. Be blessed.

7

We took a break. *Anant* and *Sakshi* showed me around the *Āśrăm*. It's a small place, the main room being the meditation hall and a few rooms for those who would want to spend a few days here. From the terrace all I could see were farms and trees. It was exceedingly cold. We sat down on the lawn, where the sun beams began to defrost me.

"Those who witness movement of time and creation know what the future will bring about." *Anant* who is *Bapuji's* son began to speak. "Scientists say that there was no concept of time before the Big Bang. When the concept of time began, that's when the Big Bang occurred. There was a great big blast and the elements and all other things like planets, etc… came out gradually and we were then slowly able to see all this. But where did the soul come from? Why is the soul not to be seen? That is the point. *Bapuji* wants to tell us about those things that cannot be seen and the *Gītā* too says that 'what is not to be seen is the Truth and what can be seen is perishable'. The divine body of Light that we had, the power of *Kṛiṣna* who had the divine body that enabled Him to lift a whole mountain with His little finger; what was the proportion of *Paṛam* elements in His body, and how much is it now? Our hair begins to turn gray at the age of thirty and youngsters suffer from arthritis, diabetes, heart issues, exhaustion, insomnia, all illnesses associated with senior citizens, so what is really missing? What elemental energy is missing within us now that young men and women are falling ill, getting grey hair, getting heart attacks and other ailments that one associates with old age? Can you imagine what will happen to our children and grand-children, twenty and forty years from now? We need to immediately increase the level of prime elements within the cosmos and within us otherwise the future will be totally grim." *Anant* spoke to me in *Gujarati*.

"So how do we increase the level of *Paṛam Taṭvas*?" I inquired.

"There is just one way to increase our *Paṛam Taṭvas*. It is to increase our *Sañkalp Śaktis* or the purity of our intentions and thoughts. As each philosophy has its own reasons for germination and it is based on the need of the hour, we too need to get our act together. If we remain tied to the old thought patterns and ways then we will not find salvation. For instance, see what happened to the *Somnath* temple? *Bhagwan Chandra* or the Lord of the Moon had made the *Somnath* temple to release Himself from a curse. *Chandra Dev* was the first one to start paying obeisance to Lord *Śiva* in this Temple. His prayers were accepted and He attained freedom. But times changed and scores of people have worshipped at the *Somnath* temple but what happened to them? Did Lord *Śiva* come down for them? The *Mughals* who arrived in India attacked and looted the *Somnath* temple of its wealth seventeen times. At that time no God came down as a Saviour. Currently, the scenario is such that people steal precious idols, cash and ornaments from temples. Till now no God has come to save the temple from being robbed. So, now it is clear that no one is going to come down to save our places of worship. There is no saviour who will come to save the earth. Earlier when *Śivji's* temple was built and He was remembered, He came to save His devotees. But now, does Lord *Śiva* come down to save His own temples from being robbed? No.

Why? Because the purity in the five elements that existed in those days is missing; the elemental-forces then and now are completely different and lack the prime and pure elemental force within each element. One thing is clear, that we have come down to Mother Earth to complete our Karmas. But how will our Karmas be completed if we keep getting sucked into committing more Karma? Whenever, we do anything good or bad, our Karmas, positive or negative increase."

I don't agree with this sentence. When we perform any action with the motive of expectation then our Karmas increase; good or bad, but if our actions aren't motivated by results, but just by giving our best to life and those around us, without expecting gain or favour, then we aren't Karma bound. For example, if you help an individual with the motive of even gaining blessings or balancing your Karmas, then you have got sucked into the vortex of give and take and karmic bondage. The realm of Karma is exceedingly subtle. Often in channelling *Bābā Sai* has guided that it is easier to pass a camel through the eye of a needle than an individual to pass through life without karmic entrapment. Thus, when you even help another person, do so because you can't see the person miserable or hungry or sick or suffer; once you go beyond seeking even blessings and gratitude and words of praise and a pat on the back from one's Master, then you go beyond karmic give and take. Thus, it's not about good and bad, it's about intentions and motives for doing what's good and bad; get rid of intentions and motives and expectations and just give your best to life, your Master and release and save yourself from hurt, sorrow, heartache, karmic bondage. Just remember one thing, release yourself from constantly being in a state of expectation. Every thought, action, word, need not have some kick-back; some advantage; something in it for you or me. Seeking any kind of reward is an exercise in tortuous futility as you are then bound to the laws of Karma. Back to *Anant*.

"If we leave our house then too there is a Karma that works behind the scene, and if we meet someone then too there is a Karma that takes place. So this Karma keeps on increasing and increasing endlessly."

"So how do you end this cycle of Karma?" I inquired.

"*Bapuji* says that all our Karmas of each and every lifetime are recorded within our aura. The only way to erase the recording within us that has accumulated over thousands of years and countless of lifetimes is to recall continuously the Divine nature of the *Paṛam Ātmā* - the Creator; what you may call as Light or Radiance or Brightness. No God or Goddess can absolve us of our Karmas. The only way to achieve karmic absolution is to go within ourselves and meditate on the *Paṛam Ātmā*. Now we call Him, *Paramātmā,* or God but it actually is *Paṛam Ātmā,* The Original Supreme One, who has created us. Recall Him with our intellect placing Him beyond the universe, beyond the Big Bang, beyond crores or trillions of light years away."

"You mean visualize oneself back into the Great Flame or The Creator. Through meditation and visualization and affirmation become One with the Creator and achieve the state of *Aum Tat Sat* or I Am That?" I inquired.

"Yes. No other way is possible. And if we reach there, then we become one with the Creator and only then will we be truly absolved of all Karma and give and take."

"So this is possible only through meditation, visualization and affirmation?" I inquired.

"Yes, only through meditation. *Bapuji* has uploaded a video on youtube.com with similar thoughts called 'I am the Messenger'. In that he has mentioned that on earth various people came at various times to basically give mankind a message of Oneness. They have tried to give Their message to one and all. Like, *Jesus Christ* who came and said that 'I am the Messenger and God is Light'. But They have all given Their Message and left and gone away and have not returned to earth as They know that no one is going to listen to Them anymore. So now we are on our own. *Bapuji* wants us to reach that Place where even Time didn't exist."

"Once again repeat the process for me." I knew the process but knowing me and my readers, it's best to be safe than sorry.

"It's the same thing when we sit for meditation. Firstly, we see ourselves in the form of light. Imagine your whole body within like the brightness of the sun, and then slowly start to move upwards, above the earth and beyond the Milky Way. Move further across the infinite-trillions-of-crores of creations. There exists the Bright Light which is the *Paṛam Māhā Brāhṁā*. It is the same *Jyotir Brāhṁ*, which *Bapuji* refers to, from which the whole creation was created. We reach there right in front of It. We are standing right there in front of the Light. The Light is like a trillion Suns in One; extremely bright and purely white. We take-in the Light and its power and disperse it to the entire universe through our Light Body. Just like the sun's rays take about eight minutes to reach the earth, similarly we will give-out that power which we receive from the *Jyotiṛ Brāhṁ* and give it to the world. And then add into it pure intentions or *Sañkalps*. Intentions or *Sañkalps* like 'get up, awaken, it is time to transform the elements, it is time to recognize the *Paramātmā*' and we also put the *Sañkalp* that awakens the Gods, just like the Sages or *Ruśis* earlier used to conduct many great *Yagyās* to awaken the Gods."

So the way I understand is that once you are standing in front of the Great Flame, it is important to consistently affirm a pledge or send out a message. It could be a simple message like, 'let there be peace and joy in all of creation' or 'let all live in contentment and laughter' or 'let all realize their Godhood and the self-realization of Oneness'; or 'wherever *Ruzbeh* lives, let smoking be permissible in all cafes and restaurants'. I guess you have got the gist.

"On planet earth when we offer something to the Fire in the *Yagyā,* it finally is five-elemental in nature. What we want is the Supreme Element or *Paṛam Taŧva,* in our soul. Only the message of the *Paramātmā* can enter directly and that's when the soul awakens. Whatever element the soul is made from, the soul will accept only that element." *Sakshi* informed.

"But how do you work on your already built-up Karma? Merge yourself with the Great Flame and then all Karmas dissolve...?" I inquired.

"Yes, exactly!" Replied *Sakshi.*

"But what about our daily Karmas? One cannot escape from performing those?" I inquired.

"Doing our daily chores is fine, but getting entangled in it and then the occurring Karma is not the right state for us all. When we talk about bringing about a transformation, then it is this human body that can bring about transformation or change in the self and in the world. The three-elemental body or the spirit cannot bring about this change. It is only in the human body, in the five-elemental stage that not only can you understand the ancient wisdom, but you also have the capability and the platform to do something about it. One can understand knowledge and after understanding, transform the knowledge into Divinity and Godhood. That understanding only a human will have."

"So what you are saying is that the Spirit cannot achieve this? Why?" I inquired.

"You are right, a spirit cannot achieve this. If we now talk about *Kṛiṣna* or any other God or Gurus who have dropped Their bodies, They are present in this world, either in the spirit form or the three-elemental form. They are helping Their devotees. They are in the spirit world helping Their lot. But They cannot bring about a change and transformation, because even in the *Gītā* it is written that 'this body is priceless'. When you are born as a human, you have an innate understanding to know yourself, to understand the world and the drama. How do we do away with our Karmas if we do not have a body? If a spirit wants to convey to you and wishes to talk to you, how will it convey to you its thoughts? If it wishes to talk to you or discuss knowledge with you, what will it do and how will it do that? It will need an instrument, won't it? It will need a channel to convey its thoughts. The spirits need a medium or a channel or a vehicle or a vessel. So this body is an invaluable instrument to finish our Karmas. It is with the body that relations are born, and our future work is done."

"But a lot of philosophies say that after you pass over, you go up and you enjoy the good Karma and then come down, so how do you…"

"But they can enjoy the fruits of their Karma themselves only. So when a soul leaves its body, it takes along with it all the good Karmas that it has done on this earth and takes knowledge with it. The soul can only keep the knowledge to itself and not share the knowledge."

"What good is that knowledge which is not for the good of all?" I mused aloud.

"Exactly! That is why all good souls take birth again and again to share their knowledge and bring about good in the cosmos and to those around them and then they go back. Their work is over. Those who wish to believe are free to believe and the ones who wish to get further entangled in their Karmas can carry on. There are many Gurus and Masters who speak through the television that they have the blessings of a particular Master Soul and that they are spreading the teachings and message of that Great Soul. But that means that Master Soul too needs an instrument and that the Spirit cannot do anything by itself. If the Spirit could do anything then It would not need instruments to convey messages and get things done. That is why being born as a human being is so important. If you wish to be free from the bondage of Karma, then one must only do such Karmas where you are not bound or attached. Wisdom is one such thing. Whenever we teach anyone or explain the *Jñān*, then we do it selflessly or *Nih-Swarth*. Now we wish to get all the knowledge into a book; there is no selfish motive in the same. Your readers should understand the knowledge, understand themselves and involve themselves in the transformation of the World; that is our sole purpose. So in such an action I am not getting into bondage of Karma with anybody. There is no relationship being created between me and the reader. So if I wish to go beyond Karma then there are two things that play a part: first is lifestyle, where through one's own self and one's desires we release oneself from the web of Karma and secondly, are our thoughts, desires or intentions to bring about good in creation. I can wish for more material pleasures and possessions or I can wish and intent on peace, harmony, love amongst all in creation.

"So when the individual brings about a ruling and controlling power over its intentions or thoughts, the aura and atmosphere around the soul and its body will change significantly. Today, if I make a positive *Sañkalp*, then the souls that surround me also will be of my same wavelength. So the more I keep reigns over my thoughts – a ruling and controlling power over what I think – it shall bring about an increase in my *Ākāś Tatva* or the Ether or Space element within me. *Ākāś Tatva* is symbolic of Silence within me. If one has more Silence of the soul, it obtains more power of the *Ākāś Tatva*. This *Tatva* of Silence is a kind of energy. With more Silence the proportion of the other four elements and composition of all five elements in the body changes. That's when one begins to draw more power. More Silence signifies more Space or Ether Element which in turn indicates more spiritual power."

"So what is the best way of going about achieving this state where you increase the *Ākāś Tatva* or the power of Silence?" I inquired.

"You tell me? How will you increase Silence within?"

"By getting married?"

Anant sported a big grin which disappeared by a mere *Ākāś-Tatvic* glance by his wife.

"The best way is to silence the mind." Answered *Sakshi*. "The control you have over your thoughts will increase the amount of *Ākāś Tatva* in you, which is nothing but symbolic of silence and vacuum. If that space energy inside increases then the power within you to manifest your thoughts into reality will increase. Miracles take place when this power increases and manifestation takes place of all that you want and by then the only thing you will want is divine peace for yourself and for all of creation. So, first of all we have to make ourselves an 'energy body' – a source of energy. Two things have to be in tandem, reduce creating further Karmas and control your thoughts. Bring about Silence within you. Increase the *Ākāś Tatva* or Space or Vacuum within you, so that the power and the *Sañkalp Śaktis* rise within you. Then whatever we think will happen. So when we talk about the 'transformation of the elements', which is the crux of our philosophy, the driving force is to bring about divine peace and eternal happiness.

"We know the elements are changing on earth. We have to now refine the elements in nature. And how can they be refined? If we impart knowledge to one-and-all, then they can bring about transformation with their thoughts and intentions or *Sañkalps;* but they need to be given precise knowledge. *Bapuji* says that the Creator does no harm or good to anyone. He or She is neutral. Then how is this world turning into such a negative place? *Paramātmā* is not doing all of this. We always blame Him and say: 'Oh God what have you done or why are You doing this to me?' It is not God who is doing anything, but it is through our Karma that we are experiencing good or bad times. The doer is us. So our philosophy is such that if the correct direction be given to all, and people start meditating the way they should and start filling themselves up with divine silence and try their level best not to get tangled up in too much Karma then ultimately we will create a world that will be peaceful and happy."

"You mean go about life doing your duty but not getting entangled or attached to it or the consequences."

"Yes *Ruzbeh*. There is no other way. The other main crux of our philosophy is that we are in search of the 108 Seed Souls. Why 108, for it is a chain of events. So, these 108 Seed Souls whose *Sañkalps* are running the world – through their controlling power on their creations' thoughts and *Sañkalps* – bring about peace and divinity to all their creation and to all of creation. Till you don't go deep within yourself, how will you know whether you are one of the main Seed Souls? So if these 108 Seed Souls realize their energy and if they are made to understand about transformation of elements and that they can work upon the same through their thought powers, and in this particular way bring energy into the world and transform the world, then our work is done."

"So basically anybody can be one of the 108 souls, which means everybody should assume they are one of the 108 souls, and meditate and bring about world transformation. Which means to bring about world change, or change in creation, in reality is in the hands of each and everybody. Okay, now let us say that we have someone reading this book and that person says that 'I also can be one of the 108, now what do I do?' how does that individual go about doing this?" I inquired.

"First of all he or she needs to be filled with knowledge. Reason being, it is imperative to have knowledge..."

"The purpose of this book is to impart that knowledge. The person is reading the book, so expects the knowledge to be in the book... what is the first step to move towards world peace and to spread divinity? Knowledge is there in the book. Now what does he or she do?"

"Meditation is the most important thing, and you need to plug into that Power House, as, if you won't plug in, the energy will not be supplied."

"Let us say *Sakshi*, that he is sitting somewhere in Czechoslovakia. He is the normal common man, goes to work, comes back but always believes that he too can contribute to bring about positive change in the world, in the cosmos, and he is not going to come to India to meet *Bapuji*... let us assume that. He doesn't even know the language. Okay? The book has been translated, he has read it and he says, now what do I do? Now, for someone who is sitting so far away, what can be done? This is very important. Because a lot of readers might say that if I can help creation, let me do my bit... what is the first step? How does he or she start? Should the person first start to meditate on being one with the Great Flame or the Creator? Then infuse himself or herself with the Energy and then spread the Light to all of creation with the right kind of affirmations? Also increase the element of Space or Silence within so that there is more power within and then with that power, bring about the intent or *Sañkalps* to create harmony and peace in all of creation?" I looked at both of them. *Anant* cleared his throat.

"Yes. That's the only way."

Mataji had joined us and was listening silently.

"*Betā* in the Divine Form there is a body of Divine Light or *Divya Pŗakāś*. This sunlight gives us warmth, life and heat, right? But the Divine Light gives us peace and divinity. It cannot burn you. It is a different light. So in the body of Divine Light, we have to stay in the *Sūkśm Vatan*. It means *Sūkśm Duniyā*."

"And what does *Sūkśm Vatan* or *Duniyā* mean?"

"*Sūkśm* means subtle and *Vatan* means a place to live. The Sublime Abode or Subtle or Astral World. Space, speed and time of each place is different. Space, speed and time at this moment is different from what it was a century ago or what it will be a year from now on. Each place and dimension, it is different. Up there, in the subtle world, we have to create a statue or *a Rūp*, a form, an image of yourself, just like you are in your exact form down here. And going into that, you have to make your affirmations. Remember when we talk about a finite point of beginning, we say *Hud* or limit. Where does the 'accountable' Limit begin? It is 150 *Arab Pŗakāś* Years or 150 Trillion Light Years away where we can say is the beginning of the *Ākāś* or Ethereal element. During meditation you have to go beyond even that, still beyond that where the Absolute Authority is present, you create a form of yourself there; a ditto image of yourself."

"I have to truly believe that I am up there isn't it?"

"You are up there! Yes." Affirmed *Mataji*.

"Your light body, it's your satellite." Added *Sakshi*.

"*Beta* the creation is through intentions. Whatever we have thought before is then translated and created in the five-elemental world. Whatever was there in our *Sañkalp* can be seen in front of us today. So why cannot we make a New World with our *Sañkalps*? These destructible things that you see all around you is what we have created. We have created destructible things, so then why cannot we make things that are *Şāşwat* as well? *Şāşwat* means necessarily permanent and that which lasts forever. It also means *Vināś-heen* or that which cannot be destroyed and is essentially eternal. The moment you really begin to stay longer up there, all our *Sañkalps* and karmic bonds begin to dissolve or they get burnt away. Remember that son, it will happen! You will not even remember anything. Like we generally get *Sañkalps* and remember things from here and there... all that too will end. But the flip-side is that after gaining so much power through this method of visualization and meditation, if we desire something, then we will get caught in those desires or intentions. And all those who have come through you will also get caught in those same intentions. But the more you remain in that limitless form and Beyond-the-Beyond, rays will emerge from within us just like from the Sun 'beams or rays' emerge. But this Sun is nothing in front of you then because you are limitless and this Sun who gives us light, life and warmth, still is tangible and is not infinite but you are infinite because you are now in the Beyond of the Beyond. The ideal intention or *Sañkalp* that needs to be made is: *'In the World of the Finite and the Infinite, let Infinite Paṛam, Paṛam, Paṛam Sukh Śānti or Supreme Joy and Peace Prevail'*. When the vibrations of supreme joy and peace will flow down, all souls that are here and even in the world of the three elements, in all the worlds whether seen or not seen, all will slowly begin to experience supreme joy and peace. You become like a magnet. When the cosmos gets this power of the magnet, it will awaken too and take knowledge from you. And slowly all those who have come through you will begin to work towards transforming the world."

It did make sense. All is created by thought; the Supreme Thought. Become one with the Supreme and all that you think too shall be created. Just as fire can never be corrupted, similarly, once you are one with the ultimate Rock Star, only profound music can emerge.

"If we want *Śakti* or power or energy then where will we get it from? Inquired *Mataji*.

"From the Beyond-the-Beyond-the-Beyond. From the original *Bāp* or *Bhai* of all things." I answered.

"Yes. We have emerged and come out from there. We need to focus only on the Absolute Authority. All that you seek, go up there and it will be given to you first hand. You don't need it from anybody else. Yes, the Path needs to be shown. How to get up there needs to be shown but afterwards all one needs is to merge oneself with the Absolute Authority and you will have everything from the Source. What kind of knowledge do we want? We want knowledge about the One from whom we have come and emerged. When He will give us knowledge, only then it will be understandable to us. Take a simple word like *Upvās,* in English you would call it fasting. *Upvās* means *'Upar Vās Karna Hai'* or To live Up There. Where do we have to go? It is all above. When you will see *Bapuji* preaching or teaching you will wonder whether his mind is a mind or a computer. He will elaborate upon all and tell us all automatically in points. And everyone would wonder how he tells all? He has Divine Vision. And that no one else has. But when will we get the Divine Vision? When we will be in the *Divya Swarūp* and we will become worthy of it, that's when we will be granted the Divine Vision.

"*Betā* earlier the elements of *Jal* and *Prithvi* or Water and Earth were barely one per cent. We were so light that we could fly. It is written in all our scriptures how we'd fly. We were physical yet with more energy and thus we could fly. Just recently on the Discovery Channel it was broadcasted that *Māyāvi* or Alien people would come from up above and do so-and-so things. We call aliens *Māyāvi* which means those with supernatural powers. I am not talking about spirits, I am talking about aliens. So they would come down on earth and with ease move mountains and other things... now these aliens come from other planets. They have their own physical structure and elemental set up. Imagine physical beings have so much power then how much power would spirit beings have. We are also aliens – if you consider it like that. We have come to change the universe. We are also, if considered from a different perspective, aliens of a kind; but Good Aliens coming from a Good World. And, we too have come to bring about change and transformation in the world. We have not come to eat and drink here. We have come here to improve and benefit the whole world. So now you know that on earth itself we had a body that could fly. Remember in every star that exists is a world of its own. Now the ones who created various stars through intentions are down here as human beings. But unknowing to them itself, the star is run through those individuals. The one who thinks, doesn't his vibration spread across the world? *Sañkalps* spread through thoughts at the speed much faster than light."

"So what you are trying to tell me is that if the One who created Jupiter, is now either in the five-elemental stage or three-elemental stage, begins to think negatively then Jupiter planet begins to broadcast negative vibrations and if he or she thinks positively then the planet begins to spread positivity?" I asked.

"Yes *betā*. This is the power of thought and intentions."

"So each one of us represents something somewhere in the cosmos and each one has the power to magnify positivity or negativity via thoughts and intentions?" I inquired.

They all nodded in the affirmative.

"And if all souls understand their very own power and responsibility and concentrate their energies, peace will prevail." Informed *Sakshi*.

"*Betā* first was the Absolute Authority. Then came

the *Bayhuđ na Paṛam Pitā* or the Founding Father of the Infinite. The Mother was next. The seven sages or *Sapt Ruśis* followed. The seven notes of music, seven days of the week, seven oceans on earth, seventh dimension, seven chakras, all this came through Them, so the seven souls are the *Jñān Sāgar* or oceans of knowledge. After that there were twelve more souls created. We have twelve *Rāśis* and twelve months in a year. Then came the twenty-four; gold is twenty-four carat in purity, twenty-four-hours make a complete day. This way the first 108-souls came about; the 108-beaded rosary that each religion propagates to pray upon is in their blessed memory. These souls have served the world and worked towards benefiting the world greatly or for *Viśwa Kalyān*. That is why, Their memory remains. They have accomplished great work. They know the Supreme Authority and recognize Him and use the knowledge to work for the upliftment of the whole world. Their memory is in bringing about change and transformation in the whole world. That is why their memories have been etched. They have done immense amounts of great work.

"What is this knowledge – it's the knowledge of killing oneself; the knowledge of dying when alive. So how does one die when alive? The real death will be when you will be in this state: *'Naṣhto mohā, samruti labhḍā, ichchā mātra vidyā'*; which means, 'That person will have no wish, want; will be a *Vairāgi,* disenchanted and unattached'. The person will have everything yet will be a *Vairāgi.* So this stage follows *Bhakti;* even in the *Gītā* it is said that after *Bhakti,* one gets knowledge. And with knowledge one gets *Vairāgya* or disenchantment and detachment." Informed *Mataji.*

So basically the fact of the matter is that all those who really want to bring about positive and everlasting change in creation, need to send positive affirmations and believe that the cosmos will magnify and spread the positive vibrations to all of creation. If done with meditation I guess the results will be a thousand-fold more powerful.

I needed a smoke. On the pretext of taking an important phone call, I left the *Āśrăm*, sat under a tree, on a very ragged stone, and smoked a few cigarettes thanking whoever gave the *Sañkalp* of creating cigarettes. God Bless Him.

8

After the smoke I was taken to meet *Bapuji*. We were in his room. I sat on the bed with him, while others, sat on chairs around us. *Bapuji* made sure I had a blanket around me and a thug cap on my head.

"So in the *Tatvas*, first came Ether or Space, then Air, then Fire. From the element of Air, the element of Fire or *Agni Tatva* is created. The one that manifests in the physical gross world has its cause in the subtle. The reason for all physical is subtle. And the reason for the subtle is the subtlest or the most-subtle world. The Air element encompasses the fire element as well. From hydrogen the gas helium is created, am I right? H_2 is converted to H_3, right?"

Ya right. If I knew all this I wouldn't have plugged in the 9th standard so confidently.

"So without *Vāyu*, you cannot have *Agni*?" I wanted as-quickly-as-possible to move away from the topic of helium.

"We have fire inside *Vāyu*, where it generates electricity?"

"So what you are trying to tell me is that if there is no Air, then there will be no Fire?"

"Yes. That is why the *Vāyu Tatva* has been created before *Agni*. Initially, how were the elements created? They were created because *Sañkalps* had begun. As *Sañkalps* started, first came *Paṛam Ākāś* or Divine Ether from which came *Paṛam Vāyu* or Divine Wind or Air from which came *Paṛam*

Agni or Divine Fire. (For the record now, now we have just Ether, Air, Fire, in the five-elemental world, 'Divine' or *Paṛam*, is no longer present in the elements.) For instance, we all have heard of ancient musicians who through certain *Rāgās* (ancient Indian musical compositions), would bring down the rain, or light oil lamps called *diyās*. When the *Dēpak rāgā* would be played or sung, the power the music generated would light lamps and the *Malhār rāgā* rendered would get the rain down. So, actually inside the element of Air, the element of Water is also present. H_2O is the formula, right? It is the merging of hydrogen and oxygen – the constitution of the elements of water. H_2O is made from *Vāyu*."

"There is water in the Air element, that is obvious but fire too is in the Air element…"

"Yes *betā*. So water and fire both are in the Air element which is in the Space element or in the element of Ether. The earth is the combination of all elements. So then gradually as all elements came into being, the *Ātmās* began to multiply. And as the power started to dwindle, the distinction between man and woman started to take place.

"Our scriptures say that there are *Anant Koti Brāhmāñḍs* in existence. Which means there are countless or trillions of galaxies and that trillions of creations are made and destroyed from time to time. If there are trillions of galaxies according to the scriptures, then logically that means there are *Anant Koti Śivas* or infinite crores of *Śivas* too. So there are *Śivas* and then there is *Māhā, Māhā, Māhā Śiva* – the Absolute Authority. That's why we celebrate *Māhāśivrātri* once a year, even though *Śivrātri* comes every month.

"*Śiva* made the world of the five gross elements from the Divine Elements. He takes the whole creation into Himself just as in science they say the Black Hole engulfs millions of creations into its belly. Why are we unhappy? The main reason is that the five elements that make us, have got polluted and filled with negativity. The air we breathe and the water we drink is all polluted. This is bound to affect our emotional, mental, physical state. There will come a time when man will go beyond the five elements to survive. The world and the vibrations therein will turn from gross to subtle and go higher. When there is utter darkness only then the bright sunlight of knowledge can enlighten you and one will get direct knowledge from the Source. The whole world will be of only subtle bodies. The need for physical bodies will end.

"This happens once and only comes through the One. The divinity of the Ultimate Father comes through the way He imparts knowledge. How do you know that the Father is the Ultimate Authority and the right one? Through the awakening of the *Third Eye Chakra*; and that is gained through meditation. He gives us the knowledge of the New World. We have come from *Amar Lok* or from immortality to *Mrutyu Lok*, the land of death. How was the world created? Where are the deities? How was our soul created? All these answers one can get via *dhyān* or meditation.

"When Lord *Kṛiṣna* came down to earth, what did He say? He said that '*this war between truth and untruth I cannot stop. This Māhābhāṛăta, I cannot stop*.' Now today, the *Devatās* or the Demi Gods have descended upon earth. Imagine Lord *Kṛiṣna* could not stop the *Māhābhāṛăta*, then who is going to be able to stop this degeneration that one sees within and all around?"

I have this eternal itch to interrupt, so here I go again. I believe that the one who goes deep within, meditates, becomes one with his or her breath, merges with his or her breath, thus becoming one with the Source and through the Source, the individual taps into the universal grid of knowledge, and thus can go beyond man and become superman or as earlier days we would say become God-like.

The Māhābhāṛăta really is within one self. The five brothers or *Pāndavās* stand for five senses. The day you bring your five senses under control; the innumerable emotions and desires – one can call them *Kauravās* – seize to have a hold on you and you are free to soar. The problem is that this is so simple to achieve that most of us are never going to achieve it as we have lost all respect for simplicity and are into designer stuff; be it designer meditation, healing, cults, religions… the old fashioned simple stuff, doesn't appeal to us anymore. So yoga has to become power yoga and steam yoga and meditation has become to have various fancy names added to it and Pranic healing has to become some fancy Italian-worded form of healing, as the simple stuff of sitting in a corner, going within, becoming one with the Breath, is not in vogue any more. You can dress a horse in a Ralph Lauren Limited Spring Collection Edition, the fact remains it is still going to be a horse and is never going to clean-up after crapping all over the place. Look everywhere and most people have become spiritual shoppers when the answer truly just lies in going within. Focusing on the breath or one's Master, and becoming one with the Breath and Master. Ok, enough of my mumbo jumbo.

"Only the one who knows the knowledge of creation can inform about the destruction of this world. The elements need to be converted now. It is time that this happens. The knowledge of *Viśwa Parivàṛtăn* or changing the world and the *Parivàṛtăn* or transformation of creation is most important. It is present in the *Śāstṛās* but not yet imparted by anyone." Continued *Bapuji*.

"Now what will happen? What do we have? We have our soul. We need to connect with the One with divine vision and divine knowledge to go about this transformation from a state of death to a deathless or immortal state. We want to bring into the world *Paṛam Taṫvas* and Divine

Light. The transformation has to come about converting the elements. The only way is to meditate, visualize and become one with the Absolute Authority. Then through the power of affirmations and visualizations bring down the Prime Elements and spread it through all creation.

"We talk about the planets and days of the week and also pray to various Gods. So if a soul has come from one of the Seed Souls who has created a planet, then all the qualities of the Seed Soul along with the planet gets infused into the individual. So, this is the world of *Devatās* or Demi Gods and made by the *Devatās*. So if the Gods and Goddesses imbibe this knowledge of transformation and create *Sañkalps* or intentions and affirmations to bring about change, then They can bring about positive change in the five elements. But the problem is most of the 33-crore Demi Gods and Goddesses are here on earth as human beings. They have forgotten their power. So if They are miserable, obviously, all who have come from them will be miserable too. But if They meditate, send positive affirmations and prayers for peace and wellbeing then their creations too will become peaceful and by them becoming peaceful, their individual Creator will get more peace and power and it will have a positive effect once again on the creations. We are entangled in the five elements and to get out of that we need to recharge our bodies with light energy and recharge the cells of our bodies with divine light. *Jñān dān* which could mean spreading knowledge or educating people or even sponsoring education is *'Māhā dān' or* the greatest of all charities." Informed *Bapuji*.

Which is even in practical terms very true as you enable the individual to become self reliant; be it in the world or in spiritual growth. When an individual has the knowledge or has the road map, he or she can reach his or her destination much quicker and avoid pitfalls along the way. Like one sage smoking an extremely-questionable-looking cigarette told me, "Brother, give a chap a fish, he will eat it all day and in all probability get indigestion the next day, which is so not cool brother, not cool at all! But teach the idiot to fish and you sort-of set him up for life and for sure alter his body odour for eternity, but that's beside the point." Back to *Bapuji*.

"Our body has a subtle body and a causal body. There are seven different types of cosmic powers residing in the causal body. The cosmic energies that are there in the atmosphere automatically charge the causal body. The causal body runs the three-elemental subtle body and the subtle body runs the five-elemental gross body. Origin of all physical ailments or disease commences in the causal body.

"The causal body is made of *Paṛam Ākāś, Paṛam Vāyu* and *Paṛam Agni* elements; Prime Ether, Air and Fire elements. When the *Paṛam Ākāś Tatva* gets corrupted due to tension and stress, jealousy, lust, anger, hunger for various things, also too much of talking and gossiping, we suffer from all types of serious diseases. And the deficit of the *Paṛam Ākāś Tatva* causes most of the diseases. First the disease attacks or gets ingrained into the causal body. That is because it's the first layering of one's body and also the most subtle. Closest to the soul is the *Paṛam Ākāś Tatva*, then *Paṛam Vāyu Tatva* and then *Paṛam Agni Tatva*. When the individual increases his or her wants and desires; he or she gets agitated and screams and shouts and becomes restless, becomes more outwardly, then there is an imbalance in the *Paṛam Ākāś Tatva* which is responsible for peace and calmness within oneself. So that's why the Sages would close their eyes and be in their *Divya Swarūp* or their Divine State only. There is a chain reaction when the *Paṛam Ākāś Tatva* is affected; it affects the *Paṛam Vāyu* and *Paṛam Agni Tatvas* as well. That is why the causal body is called Causal for it is caused and reacts by our *Sañkalps* or desires or intentions. What is the solution for this corruption within the causal body *betā*?"

"Go within. Meditate. Be calm. Be in peaceful, joyous and positive surrender to whatever the Master has in store for you while still giving life your hundred per cent." I replied. Or just get sloshed, I mused.

"Yes. Now the subtle body was made due to the deficit in the *Paṛam Tatvas* in the causal body. There was a deficit of fifty-per cent of *Paṛam Tatvas* in *Brāhṁāpuri* or the land of *Brāhṁā*. Why? As the *Devatās* or Demi Gods used-up the power of the soul to run *Brāhṁāñḍs* or galaxies that they had created. Thus there was an imbalance in the *Paṛam Ākāś Tatva,* resulting in imbalance in the *Paṛam Vāyu Tatva* and then the *Paṛam Agni Tatva*. The imbalance in the *Paṛam Agni Tatva* affected the structure at the atomic level or the 'atom' or *'aṇu'* level of all elements. So the atoms or the *'aṇu'* of the *Paṛam Ākāś, Vāyu* and *Agni Tatvas* all got affected. In each cell and around the atoms there are the *Paṛam* elements of *Ākāś, Vāyu* and *Agni;* each of them inside every cell. The gross elements are the result of the deficit in the *Paṛam Tatvas*. Now the reason is the presence of the Black Cosmic Energy in the atmosphere. Only one-per cent is Golden Cosmic Energy and 99 per cent is Black Cosmic Energy. So virtually 100 per cent of the atmosphere is corrupted. When the *Ātmā* or soul or the individual performs *Yog* or meditation, very often it misfires, even though the intention is right, due to the corruption of the *Tatvas,* negative *Sañkalps* have started to come about. One has to be really selfless to perform *Yog* or meditation and not have a single selfish or self-centred thought, as during *Yog* what you think will come about. When one performs *Yog,* and it's not completely selfless and not for the cosmic good of all, what happens is that instead of the golden cosmic rays going into his soul, black cosmic rays enters the soul.

"What is Black Cosmic Energy made of? In the causal body there are seven different types of cosmic powers. Powers like the characteristics of the planet *Śukra* or Mercury, and so-on-and-so-forth... similarly, the seven main Creators who are there – through their *Sañkalps* going wrong, the Black Cosmic rays are created. There are seven main Creators, through whose *Sañkalps* the cosmos was created. That is why there are different colours of the causal body. The causal body is a combination of all colours.

"So when one performs *Yog*, and says *Aum*, the sound vibrations of *Aum* affect the causal and astral bodies and then through that the physical body too. *Aum* means *Brähṁā, Viśnu* and *Mahesh*. But the problem is most people are praying to the *Brähṁā, Viśnu* and *Mahesh*, of this Creation, and not the Absolute Authority and the Seed Soul of the Founding Father of the Infinite. The Trinity of this galaxy does not have power anymore and have become humans. So, earlier when one would chant *Aum* the power would come from the Main Authority as earlier the sages knew that one had to go right back to the main Source and not pray to just the Gods of one particular *Brähṁāñḍ* or galaxy.

"A lot of people are doing *Pṙāṇāyam* but there is more of carbon dioxide and carbon monoxide in the air, so the *Vāyu Taŧva* in the Subtle body will reflect the negative and cause imbalance in the *Paṛam Vāyu Taŧva* and that will affect the *Ākāś Taŧva* and thus the soul will also be affected. The entire imbalance is caused due to the imbalances in the causal body only."

I do not agree with this. *Pṙāṇāyam* according to me is the conversion of all elements into *Pṙāṇā*, the life spark, or in *Bapuji*'s lingo, converting normal *Taŧvas* into *Paṛam Taŧvas.* Yes, it is important that when you do *Pṙāṇāyam* you visualize golden light entering you and the dark elements within one being exhaled. Once this takes place, one can squeeze out *Prāṇā* even from carbon dioxide and monoxide. Every element has *Prāṇā* and through one's intentions one can infuse oneself with true cosmic energy.

"The *Vāyu Mandàḷ* or atmosphere was good around three-hundred years prior… that's why they used to teach *Prāṇāyam* so that the cosmic oxygen would go into the body and earlier they would be in a *Nih-Sañkalp* state. Maximum problems arose due to tensions that caused *Sañkalps* to move faster and that caused the *Paṛam Ākāś Tatva* to deplete. That's how the causal body lost its power.

"All the recordings of your previous births or *Sanskārs* that include experiences and conditioning are in the causal body. It is in the seventy-five-thousand crore cells causal body and the cells are made of what? *The Paṛam Tatvas.* The *Paṛam Tatva* body is the causal body that covers your soul. But now in the causal body also there is a lot of black cosmic energy. Why did the corruption in the *Paṛam Tatvas* happen? Why did the *Devatās* turn into human beings? Why did those staying in the *Divya Swarūp* or image of God and *Divya Lok* or heaven become human beings?

"When someone plays music he or she uses the seven notes to create music. Seven notes means seven colours. When *Tansen* performed the *Dēpak rāgā* or another musician played the same *rāgā,* there would be a vibrational change in the atmosphere due to a cosmic power that would react when the *Dēpak rāgā* would be played. The cosmic power would convert the properties in the atmosphere and that's how the *diyās* or oil lamps were lit on their own.

"But now this doesn't happen, because the person singing this *rāgā* does not have the power nor does the atmosphere have the *Paṛam Tatvas*. How was the atmosphere or *Vāyu Mandàḷ* corrupted? Any spiritual power can control the gross elements. What does the gross world depend upon? In reality it only depends upon the subtle. And the subtle depends upon the more refined subtle and even that more-refined subtle depends upon the *Nirākār* or formless Creator." *Bapuji* halted to take a sip of water.

Anant then began to speak.

"*Bapuji* speaks about the Sages who leave the world of *Moh Māyā,* or attraction and attachment and emotion to live in the woods. Relatives and the demands of the body are in the five-elemental world and they have immense strength to suck even the sages into the *Māyā* trap. So what does attraction or attachment do? It diverts your power into the object of your *Moh* or attraction and the negativity connected with the attraction or attachment enters into your own body.

"That is why they say that see in such a manner that in reality you do not see; listen in such a manner that you do not listen and live in such a manner that you are there but still not there; complete detachment from all results. Be absent from the spoken word, from the voice, from feelings and emotions. Don't be in emotion as well. Do your Karma but without emotion. *(Just butting in with my two bit…I think it means without attachment to the outcome; without emotion would make us cold, distant and zombie like. Yes, without expectation of reward, praise or outcome one could really advance.)* Work for the welfare of souls without being emotional about the whole thing, without getting pulled into the current of emotions." Informed *Anant*. *Bapuji* then continued.

"Those who live for themselves are animals. And those who live to give others happiness are *Devatās* or Demi Gods, says the *Gītā.* The one who is involved in bringing about change in the entire creation is *Bhagwan* or God. One who desires to convert all negative into positive is a Demi God. And it is with knowledge only that you can bring about change. Why are we unhappy? We are unhappy due to Karmas and having forgotten the Creator and when that happens one gets involved in further *Moh*. That's why one is unhappy even after being wealthy and healthy.

"When the quantity of *Paṛam Agni Tatva* increases in the body, it brings negativity in the subtle and physical bodies and one tends to experience anger, negativity, depression etc... And *Vairāgya Vruti*, disenchantment comes when one is silent within and outside, as one fills oneself up with more *Ākāś Tatva*. *Agni Tatva* and *Vāyu Tatva* are responsible to convert disenchantment into *Māyā* or illusion and thus get the body entangled more into the body and bodily relations.

"Thus one can make changes within one self to increase the *Ākāś Tatva* and with conscious changes of being calm within, silent, content; one can bring about subtle changes in the astral and causal levels too. One can, through one's *Sañkalps* and intentions, recall one's divine state, meditate on one's seed body, the divine body by making a satellite of oneself within the Absolute Authority. The amount of *Paṛam Tatvas* there is 100 per cent and gradually the energy will transcend and your causal and subtle body will get charged. The soul once charged, will mean all three *Paṛam Tatvas* within oneself have got balanced. Once the *Paṛam Tatvas* are balanced, the physical body will automatically become light and charged.

"Regular meditation will give temporary relief to your five-elemental body, but if we study the main cause of diseases, it is in the causal state and one needs to first focus on repairing the causal body. Once that is done, all diseases from the astral and physical body can be removed too, but only when one truly works on the causal body first. Impurity is the cause of all. And the main reason for man's downfall is that he is entangled in the attraction of body and bodily relations. So first and foremost one needs to get detached from them."

Ok, I need to add something here. Even here I feel the root cause of all issues is not attachment with the outside world but in reality attachment to yourself. In reality we love ourself the most. One needs to get detached from one's own ego. Once you get detached from your own self, worldly attachments will automatically drop-off from all the bodies. You love your child because he or she is your child. If something happens to your child you feel restless and disoriented and that makes you yearn for good health of all your loved ones as in reality your sanity and state of centeredness depends on the wellbeing of your loved ones. Take this example of a friend of mine who was head over heels in love with his dog. Whenever we met, he would keep praising the dog and shower words of endearment on the animal. If the dog was ill, this friend of mine would be depressed, worried, and a conversational shooting pain in the rectal. Then it so happened that for over a month or so whenever we met him, there was no conversation about the dog. Sometime later I got to know via his brother that the dog was put to sleep. I was a bit surprised as I used to meet my friend regularly and there was no mention about the demise of his favourite dog, who he often proclaimed to love more than his very life. The brother filled me up with what really happened. The dog got some illness in the brain. For some reason I can't fathom, the dog whenever it saw my friend it would bark loudly and rush forward trying to bite him. It once even charged and badly scratched my friend who then needed stitches. This became a routine and it reached a point that they had to tie the dog whenever my friend was at home and even then the dog would growl and bark at him. The poor dog wasn't well. It was disoriented and later on my friend insisted that the dog be put down. When I spoke to him about it he began to abuse the dog and said he didn't want to talk about it. Where did all the love and attachment for the dog disappear in two months' time?

The fact is the friend loved the dog's love and attachment towards himself. When that love and attachment turned into growls, bites and visible hate, the love went out of the window. So usually we love ourselves and through our love for ourselves we identify who we love and who we don't. Of course there are exceptions but I guess what I have seen of life, this is sort of a rule. Back to *Bapuji*.

"So become in the image of the soul. The soul is the causal body. Remember the *Paramātmā*. You will think what you see and what you think you will become. So remember your divine self while you eat, sleep, and believe that you are living in the divine land. You will gain the divine intellect and the causal body will get power. Golden cosmic light means Golden *Param Tatva*. The quantity of *Ākāś Tatva* is more in the golden cosmic zone. *Param Vāyu Tatva* is dark blue and *Param Agni* is red in colour and like that there are seven bodies inside the causal body. In an animal's soul, the amount of Black Cosmic Energy is more. Just remembering the Creator's formless state, the cosmic powers will come to you. It is important to take a *Sañkalp* where one imagines our causal and astral body first being charged and we gaining power from the Creator.

"In the three-elemental stage, there are too many *Māhā Asurs* or negative souls who reside there. What do they do in the three elements? Many crore kilometres above the earth, there are many *Asur Ātmās* or animal souls in three elements who are assembled there. They by possessing the human body eat, drink and make merry. They are *Prêt Ātmās* or earthbound souls or those who are called ghosts. They enter human bodies and quench their lust for flesh, meat and alcohol.

"Evolved souls are in a ring above them. They are the *Dharm Pitās* or religious heads and great saintly souls. More evolved than these souls, are souls in a Silence Tower which is another ring above the *Dharṁ Pitās*. As we go higher the amount of *Paṛam Tatvas* increase. On the border of this *Surya Lok* or on the border of our sun, the ring holds ten per cent of *Paṛam Tatvas*. If our causal body gets this ten per cent of Golden Cosmic Energy then our subtle body will leave our gross body and go upwards to the outer ring. In fact, even if we gain two per cent of *Paṛam Tatvas* then we will reach the outer ring. Then too we need to have the stage of *Naṣto Mohā* where all attachments are destroyed or a stage of selfless love or even a state of absolutely no desires. As we go further away from the world in circles the percentage of cosmic energy keeps on increasing because in the gross world the cosmic power is as-good-as nil. That's why; we have to go beyond this gross world. That's why when we pray or meditate or chant *Aum*, instead of gaining cosmic energy, we, nowadays tend to get Black Cosmic Energy into our system. *Sañkalps* also keep taking place when we pray, as most prayers are only further desires that we would like to be gratified. So what you ask for is tremendously important.

"If the individual thinks good thoughts then the atmosphere's one per cent Golden Cosmic Energy enters the individual's causal body. If the soul thinks creative and positive thoughts then multi-coloured cosmic energy enters the causal body. If the soul is calm, then Green Cosmic Rays enter the causal body and if anger prevails, then the atmosphere's red cosmic rays enter the causal body. Now-a-days there are souls that enter another's body and make the unsuspecting individual perform actions in either anger or lust that the individual would repent later on. He or she would keep wondering how I could have done this thing! In reality, he or she hasn't done anything. Another spirit has occupied the individual's body and performed the gory act. Likewise there are noble souls who enter physical bodies to get good work performed. These souls use the human body as a medium or a vehicle to either do good things or to spread the Light.

"If a pregnant mother thinks negatively or is filled with negative thoughts, then from the atmosphere the Black Cosmic Rays enter the child's body; thus the mother transfers Black Cosmic Energy through her ears to the child. Sometimes when a person is born, the causal body of the individual, through past life Karma may have many negative traits and thoughts. We say 'inborn nature' which actually is past life patterns and Karma showcasing in this life time. Or if the person is a great soul then the individual will come with greatness and noble traits in his or her causal and astral aura which will automatically make him or her perform noble deeds. Also an individual may have many creations of his or her own through various *Sañkalps* the individual has made and thus manifested. For instance, if the soul belongs to the 108 category, then can you imagine the number of creations that the soul will be responsible for through life times of *Sañkalps*? The soul is a Seed Soul, thus massive cosmic creations would have been created by that individual. Let us assume that he or she is responsible for over millions and millions of other souls. Now these creations are screaming in misery in their own worlds. Where do you think all their cries and misery are being absorbed? The anguish of all his creation are being absorbed in the causal and astral body of the Seed Soul who is their Creator. When all the anguish and misery of the seed soul's creation are absorbed by the seed soul, then that soul's causal and subtle body gets affected and makes the causal and subtle body negative and unhealthy. That part of the physical body which is related with the causal or subtle body gets affected badly. Also creation takes place via causal cells. The related physical part of the body gets infected, as the level of *Paṛam Taṫvas* in the causal body have got affected; this leads to paralysis, cancer and various other diseases. Let us assume the brain area of the causal body has got affected then automatically the brain area of the subtle or astral body gets affected which then leads to brain tumour, Parkinson's, Alzheimer, dementia, memory loss etc.

"How can one cure illnesses of the gross body? Through the *Mun*. *Mun* means the heart. The soul has the knowledge that it has to focus on its subtle and causal body and its divine self to gain power. But it cannot remember its divinity. Why is it so? It has the desire. It has the knowledge. But why is it unable to remember its divinity?

"Or take the example of a normal human being. Why is the soul unable to think of its subtle and divine self? It is because its intellect, mind and consciousness keeps getting attached to the demands of the body and family and friends and detractors and enemies and new cars or contracts and so on and so forth. Because the negative load caused either by past life times of karmic baggage or wrong use of Free Will or due to the agony of those whose loved ones are calling out to them; all this individually or collectively weighs down the causal body over and over again and the causal body is filled with Black Cosmic Energy. And even though one may not wish this, our mind gets diverted to the body and bodily relations due to the Black Cosmic Energy. Now imagine the plight of the Seed Soul who has millions and millions of creations in agony and are all crying out to him or her. This soul even though it does not wish, falls into the trap of negative *Sañkalps*.

"So who makes one unhappy? We know the reason and the solution of our unhappiness. In reality we have the knowledge of both. But only with knowledge one cannot get into performing *Yog*. Why? Because we keep repeatedly falling into the trap of *Māyā*. Who or what is *Māyā*?" *Bapuji* again halted to have a sip of water. He then continued.

"Relationships and family and friends are *Māyā*. If *Māyā* is present in all five-elemental things then doesn't that make our body *Māyā* too? So, when will you become *Māyājeet* or the one who has overcome *Māyā*? When will you overcome *Māyā*, as till the time you do not overcome *Māyā* or become *Māyājeet*, till then you will be unable to experience perpetual joy and happiness for this is *Mrutyulok*, and in *Mrutyulok*, one never experiences everlasting joy. If you gain joy in one *Sañkalp*, then there will be ten wishes or intentions that will give you pain. There is one per cent joy and 99 per cent pain. So with knowledge, meditation, going to the Beyond of the Beyond and praying to the Almighty, with your very being and doing your *Bhakti* sincerely and remembering the Almighty with all your heart, then from the one per cent of golden cosmic energy that is in the atmosphere, our body experiences joy and happiness. To attain peace, you have to leave your body and go back to *Divya Lok*, because you will not gain everlasting peace here. Even if the Gods have to come into the five elements, then They too will be caught up in the human form. And even though God has all the knowledge, once in the human body, He too gets caught up either in *Māyā*, or in the plight of His or Her followers."

Ok, back to my two bit. According to me *Māyā* or illusion is anything that distracts you from one's only worthwhile objective in life; merging and serving the Master and the Creator. But my take on this very controversial woman called *Māyā* is this: As long as you are never distracted from merging and serving your Master and Creator, you can go about having a blast in life and still be a *yogi*. My logic is simple. Whether you are in prayer or in a cafe, be true to yourself, being aware that your Master is with you, and be in the moment and bloody well enjoy the moment. Remember one thing, if *Māyā* is into all five-elemental things, then we are buggered whether we are eating food or drinking a good *absinthe* or malt. But so what if you are having a drink? He or she doesn't become any less spiritual than another man having boiled water. The important thing is to never forget your objective to make your Master happy and proud of you and be decent and be good and have a blast and trust me God and Master enjoy a good time. God is not some rigid accountant. Our Sages would have a rollicking time with *Somras* and *hash.* They never let go of their main priority and that is to make the Master happy and proud of them and to merge with the Old Rock Star. Now if you follow my walk, one of the two things will happen. We will all reach our Master but with a smile plastered on our face. Or we are going to get our astral asses busted but once again with a smile on our face and with a band of folks who enjoy a good life. Don't get confused with spirituality and ritual; tradition and superstition. Convert *Māyā* into a friend. Have a good time and still merge. Don't become all serious and adult. Adulthood is the root cause of indigestion, superstition, violence and boredom. Be a kid at heart. Be pure but have a blast. Yes, I agree that through meditation and visualization and affirmation, a lot of good can be done for oneself and all of creation. Spread right intentions whether you are in the physical body or you have visualized yourself with and in the Creator. Pray for peace as we really need it. People are dying in the name of God. Kids are dying because there is no clean drinking water or food. Children are being forced to beg after being put through animal like torture. The politicians, most of them, do not care for human life or human dignity. We cannot do much to make good the wrong in the physical world, but we have the power in the spirit world to do good. Through prayers and meditation and affirmations, yes, we all can in our own humble way do a lot of good for Mother Earth who has been pillaged, mutilated, violated along with most of her children who are voiceless and have no say in the larger scheme of things. Pray and wish for good and don't stop at Mother Earth but include all of creation. I firmly believe that when a child smiles, a star some place in creation, becomes slightly brighter.

Boy do I need a drink.

9

Meher and I decided to avoid leaving the room for breakfast. There were too many people around and neither of us was in a mood to change and sort of force ourselves to behave in a civilized manner. So we were on bed watching *Shaun The Sheep.* For half-an-hour we watched the programme and then in a very diplomatic tone I told her that I would now have to get up, get ready, and go to work. In *Pune,* we have a schedule and that schedule doesn't have me walking out of the room, so early in the morning.

"I have to go to work love. You have a great day, ok."

"I hate Delhi and this hotel and why do you have to go to work so early?"

"I have to love." I spoke as softly and as calmly as humanly possible as we have often had really acrimonious – or from an outsider's point of view – extremely hilarious episodes dealing with my "going-out to work" and "leaving her."

"I have to finish interviewing this Sage…"

"You and all these Sages are idiots. I hate you all. You are leaving your daughter alone… and doesn't he have a daughter to play with? Is this what you all do? Leave your children alone and work, work, work. I came down to earth for you, stayed in mummy's tummy, in that small dark place and now you leave me alone!"

An hour later, with promises of coming back early, along with various surprises, I left the hotel. Reaching the *Āśrăm* I spent a short while with *Anant* and *Sakshi* in the meditation room and then moved towards *Bapuji's* room. As usual *Bapuji* greeted me with a twinkle in his eyes and made sure I was comfortable sitting with him on bed, with the blanket draped around me, a thug cap on the old skull, a cup of hot soup in one hand and the recorder in the other and then we commenced our work.

"From 108 to thirty-three and more-crores of those created and then much more, all this creation, led to the Power of *Paṛam Taŧvas* to keep dwindling. In the initial creation of the 108 itself, one can visibly see the drop in power. The first twenty-four had more power than the remaining in the 108 and the first-eight in the twenty-four have more power and the first-three in the eight have more power and before the 108 came, the *Bayhuđ na Paṛam Pitā* who had the most power after the Almighty Authority. As the Creator of the *Paṛam Pitā* is the Almighty Authority, who has no name, *Rūp* or form and colour. *Nirākār*, God is Light, God is Light, God is Light! And what did Prophet *Muhammad* say… *'Qayāmat ke din par, Khudā Tālā, Noor Swarūp sey Dhàṛti par Khud Ayâñgâ'*; on the Day of Judgment the Almighty Lord, in His Light-form will come to earth. And why will He descend... to transform the world from its *Vyakt* or manifested form to the *Avyakt* or the non-manifested form. To achieve that, one must first of all bring down the *Paṛam Taŧva* for the priority is to bring about World Peace; *Paṛam, Paṛam, Paṛam Sukh Ṣanti* or Supreme, Supreme, Supreme Joy and Peace for tranquillity in the entire world. All of creation is burning; all are sad and unhappy. If the *Paṛam Taŧva* or Prime Elements arrive, then the entire creation will be calm. Each person needs to be given experience of the Infinite. We need them to realize that there is a soul in them. Is it *Chaitañya Swarūp* which means the All Powerful Divine Image? Are you caught-up or estranged in the five elements?" Began *Bapuji*.

"Once you are within yourself and more of a light

body, rather than the five-elemental, through meditation and silence, then the Father of the Infinite, will give you a *Suckār* or call and make you work. Like He directs all the Masters and *Māhā Yogis* and Sages and *Fakirs* and gives them direction of what is to be done for the welfare of all beings, you too will be directed as to what is to be done. This is something each one has the potential and the capability for. If I follow what He says, then all is well. If my ego comes in and I do not follow exactly as per His instructions then, my body begins to suffer.

"From up there in the *Pṛakāś Swarūp*, above the 150-Trillion light years, you need to send the right *Suckār* on earth. Along with the call or *Suckār*, you have to send the *Paṛam Tatvas,* vibrations also and focus mainly on the affirmation that: 'In the World of the Infinite Let Infinite *Paṛam, Paṛam, Paṛam Sukh Ṣanti* prevail (Let Supreme, Supreme, Supreme Divine Joy and Peace Prevail).'

"Also I do not believe that one has to eat something or not eat something or drink or not drink something to be spiritual; in the realm of the unlimited these talks of the limited need to be done away with. Whether you eat something or not or drink something or not is immaterial. Is the individual more of spirit and less of body, is all that matters and gradually he or she will stay in the Image of the Soul that's in the *Ātmā Swarūp*. Because in today's times, if one is in tension, what can that poor person do? If he eats non-vegetarian food, how does that make him or her less spiritual? Majority of the world follows a non-vegetarian diet. The big fish eat the small fish, so on and so forth. This is the way of the world. If it doesn't suit you or you do not like the idea of taking life to eat, then do not eat. One could have reached a stage where one does not want to harm anything to the best of one's capacity. We are infinite. Go beyond the finite. I know you too believe exactly in what I am saying, as I know you too do not have much of an opinion of the finite."

I smiled.

"Today's *Dharṁ* Gurus have written *'Jaisā ann, vaisā mun'* which means 'what one eats one thinks and feels'. If you want to change the complete world, then the responsibility is so huge that there are far greater things to bother about than food, alcohol, cigarettes and other things which the so-called religious scholars are against. We are trying to bring about peace in all creation, how will the food that you eat or don't eat, make any type of difference to universal peace! Without the practical experience of something most of these people advocate things. But mind you, I have never eaten non-vegetarian food. I used to drink alcohol, but the high you get from divinity no alcohol or drug can ever match-up. I left it all. Of course, I would never drink regularly. On some festive occasion I would take a peg or two, once in a while.

"You see what really matters are your intentions. Since childhood I was only concerned about how could peace and universal joy be brought into the world. Even when I was in the fourth or fifth standard I had just one agenda: 'Change the world, change the world, this world cannot go on like this.' This is what I would keep thinking and saying aloud. That's why I would go in front of *Hanumānji* and say that 'if You have the energy to lift a mountain then give it to me'. I got into serious devotion so that I could do something positive for all mankind; all of creation.

"*Hanumānji* is a super soul. He is the *Rūdra Avatār* of *Śiva* but who is the *Śiva* of this *Brāhṁāñḍ*, is something that you have to understand. He is the power of the Almighty Authority, of this world. The 11th *Rūdra Avatār* is *Hanumānji* just like *Bholay Ṣhañkar* is a part of *Ṣhiv*, or that He is a cell."

"Lot of worshippers believe that Lord *Hanumānji* is even now, present in the physical body."

"Yes *betā*, of course, He is present. He is in the three-elemental form. All *Devi Devatās* are there in three elements. Just like *Shañkar* and *Mā Pāravati*; if you go to the Himalayas, They are still there in *Mānsarovar*."

"But They are present in the three-elemental form? Which means visible to all those who are in the three elements or those who are clairvoyant?" I inquired.

"Yes. They are there in three elements, but Their power is less. All the *Devi Devatās*, whosoever have Their temples made, are present in the three elements, as the call of their devotees and children make Them stay here. Those Demi Gods or *Devi Devatās*, who have gone up in Their *Virāt Rūp* and sending positive vibrations on earth are saved from the process of being dragged down to the earth to be amongst Their disciples. Those who have realized that the best way of helping Their creations and all of creation, is not by being physically down, but by being up there and sending affirmations and healing of eternal joy and peace. With those *Sañkalps* the entire creation will benefit. But it is very difficult as the pull of the devotees bring most Masters and even *Devi Devatās* down. If for instance I remember any one of them when I am in meditation, then that person's negativity gets transferred to me and my power goes into that person, but as that person is not able to handle the power, that power is used negatively.

"Also, complete knowledge has to be given slowly and gradually, drop by drop… begin with basic knowledge, then First Be in the Image of the Soul, then Create your Divine Image, next Experience the Divine World – the *Buđhi-Siđhi* or power of Wisdom and Manifestation of Knowledge and then the *Divya Swarūp* or Divine Form, then all those who reside there and last but very importantly, think positive, never ever be negative!

"In knowledge what do we give? Just like the *Rūśimunis* would do *Tapasyā* or spiritual penance and austerity, we teach and are teaching through your book what is to be done. Soul Consciousness is a must. 'I am a spirit within this body, I am not the body.' Some are happy to focus only on their *'Iṣta Dev'* or their foremost Guru and main God. Whoever you remember, whatever He has is exactly what you will get. The question to ask is how do you know the present state of your Master or even God? What if the Master or God has been pulled down by His devotees into the five-elemental body? By remembering the Master or God who now is in the elemental body, suffering and in pain, got on by the cumulative agony of His or Her devotees, you too will receive what He or She is going through. So be careful who you focus all your attention on.

"Now you need energy, you need *Paṛam Tatva*. And the *Paṛam Tatva* is up there many trillion light years away. If your *Sañkalp* will go up there, only then will you get your *Paṛam Tatva*... You have to go right up there to fill yourself up and to disperse the *Paṛam Tatva*. Here only Black Cosmic Energy prevails but there *Paṛam Tatva* is present and if you truly want you will get even Supreme Divine Radiance. There in not even one per cent of *Paṛam Tatva* present on this earth. All around you there is black cosmic energy and if you stay as a human, you only will land up as *Jānvar Buđhi* or the one with the mentality of an animal!

"All diseases come from the heart or intention. It comes into the causal body, then the subtle body, and then filters into the physical body. Tension starts from either trying to fulfil our desires or having our desires unfulfilled. We get entangled in karmic bondage. As karmic bondage increases, tension in our soul or causal body increases too. That's when man's subtle body starts getting discharged or weakened. So when the subtle body is uncharged, that's when the gross body starts to suffer and disease comes about. Now today if you go to a doctor, he will prescribe so many allopathic medicines, which will take care of the physical aspect, but the root cause of your illness is in the subtle and causal body. And there is only one medicine for the subtle and causal body. Increase the silence within, meditate, send the right affirmations, all this will increase the *Ākāś Taŧva* and slowly the healing will take place. Medication of any sort will help the body but you have not cured the illness. It will still linger in the astral or causal body, and will reoccur, or reconvert into some other illness.

"Due to my interaction with so many people my health began to deteriorate and I got blood pressure and diabetes. I was told to take several tablets daily, which I did for a while. Later I realized the futility of it all so as time passed I used my meditation and with the power of *Yog* improved my condition. I was told to take injections for diabetes every day. But one day I stopped all medication. Doctors said that if I stopped my medication all sorts of things would happen to me. I kept quiet but intensified my meditation and now it's almost four years since I have stopped all injections and reduced my medicines to bare minimum. All I did was to charge my subtle and causal body. Now to charge the subtle body, you have to stay in the *Sūkśṃ Vatan* or the subtle world and the *Paṛam Taŧva*s need to be brought down. The problem was that as soon as I would meet someone, my channels or vibrations were so open that my power would be transferred into the person and his negativity would enter me. Even if I remember someone with my mind then, my *Buđhi* goes into him and his issues and negativity comes into me. That's why in the path of Knowledge, the *Rūśimunis* or Sages would sit in their caves and would not meet anyone. And if anyone entered into their caves, they would not like it."

I guess that is true. That Yogis would not like intrusion, is a very polite way of saying it. If anyone entered the cave of a Yogi, the poor sod of a trespasser had it. The Yogi would go all ballistic, unknot himself first, and if really upset, produce lightning and thunder, either in the cave or outside the cave, then rattle out a few curses in the common dialect, that would have an impact on the clueless chap who wandered into the cave, and all in the name of spirituality and God. Back to *Bapuji.*

"So, these sages would not meet anybody as they didn't want any transfer of aura or vibration. And I too kept falling ill and thus eventually I had to take the decision of limiting my interaction with people. So now since a few years I also sit in one room and do my *Tapasyā*. Only during *Māhā Śivarātri* do I meet people as there is a little *Jñān* left to be passed on. The fact of the matter is that more you advance in spirituality the more susceptible you become to the dangers of the five elements. Sages have auras that are over a hundred feet in diameter. Now, whoever comes into the embrace of the sage's aura will be healed and simultaneously, the negativity and dirt within their aura will be transferred into the Sage."

"How does one protect oneself?" I inquired. I mean locking oneself in a room or in a cave is the prerogative and inclination of very few people. I would go bloody nuts in a cave or a room all by myself.

"We can protect ourselves by prayers and meditation and we can seal our auras and our body, but it's not that the seal is not impregnable. Your creation is screaming and along with the screaming in each and every cell *Sañkalp*s are entering; so those *Sañkalp*s do not allow you to be sealed."

This is true. I remember my *Swāmiji Naik,* the Sage from Bangalore, the ardent child and devotee of *Mā Mookambika Devi,* on whom I was blessed with the opportunity to write the book, *The Devi's Emerald. Swāmiji* would time and again fall ill and He would worry for me too. Often, He would call me *Ruzbee* and thus He would tell me, "*Ruzbee* if you are going to jump in water you are going to get wet and no amount of protection is going to prevent Me or you from falling ill, as how much ever you protect yourself, some of those coming to Me or you are going to touch us and make us fall ill. So eat well and take care of your physical body as that is the vehicle that drives you and your soul. Now eat this fourth *Masālā Dosā* like a good boy." I miss Him a lot. In fact, one morning I woke up having a strange dream. I dreamt that I was in the *Mā Mookambika* Temple in *Bangalore*. I could see *Mā's* image and to my left was *Sai Bābā* of *Shirdi* and to my right was *Avatār Meher Bābā*. I could hear *Swāmiji*, but I could not see Him. He was as usual talking on the phone, guiding and blessing *Mā's* and His devotees; giving instructions to the staff on general upkeep of the Temple and I could hear His boisterous booming voice. He was like a Lion. So in my dream I could hear Him but couldn't see Him. I woke up and wondered about the dream and my heart sank but I sort of avoided confronting my fear. A few hours later *Murli, Swāmiji's* closest disciple, telephoned to tell me that *Swāmiji* had taken *Samādhi*.

Strange dreams, but then I've existed or lived long enough to know that life is stranger. So from my experience I have learnt that when you are in channelling or some other form of healing, the more centered you remain, the greater the chances of you being protected and your protective aura being intact. The more emotional you get the chances of you falling ill or taking on negativity (which in reality could be the suffering of those who come for help and guidance) will be much more. Vibration transfer isn't rocket science. Try to sit on a chair occupied by somebody filled with negative emotions or be in the room with such a person and you will feel disoriented, breathless, tired or uneasy; you would experience one or all these issues. That is why it is so important, whether you are a channel or a home maker, the less you get all overtly emotional and letting the small "I" rule, the greater the chances are that you will remain more centered and be able to give your loved ones, yourself and most importantly, your Lord and Master, the best of you. Caves and room service are not meant for one and all. Remember those who live in caves or are content to spend the rest of their lives by themselves in their rooms doing *Tapasyā*, have reached a point where they can leave their physical body and do astral travel at will. They know how to get their astral body out of their physical body; anytime and anywhere. So though logically they are in a cave or room, in reality, only the shell of their physical body is within, but those naughty boys are out and about, all over the place. This way, their physical body is protected from vibration transfer and still whatever work is required to be done is gone about being done in the astral dimension.

Avatār Meher Bābā often used to locate a site and His disciples would build a small hut for Him on that spot. Later on, it would be disclosed that the particular site had been a meditation place of either some Prophet or Sage. *Avatār Meher Bābā* would then stay in the hut for months, isolated from the physical world, barely eating or drinking anything, with no material comforts at all; nobody could meet Him or even see Him. His meagre one-time meal would be placed near the door and as weeks would pass, the meagre meal would become a glass of milk and then a glass of milk would become just one glass of light tea, which sufficed the *Avatār* for months. When asked why He did what He did and always in isolation; His answer was that He did more tremendous quantum and far more important work when in isolation for not only mankind but for all of creation, compared to all His physical work that He did when not in isolation. So the Masters have Their reasons. Unless you are a Master (then you wouldn't be reading this book), avoid isolation. Protect your aura via meditation and affirmations and candle, flame or sun meditation (mentioned in *The Fakir* books), and go about your life as centered as possible; and if once in a while you lose it and go all ballistic, then bloody well lose it, as we are human beings; most often a confused, self destructive lot, once in a while the scum of creation, and a few times, here and there, God personified.

"Who, as per the *Gītā,* is one's biggest enemy? The *Gītā* says that one's body and those who are in relationship with the body, i.e. one's loved ones are one's greatest enemy. And why is that? Because loved ones create further bondage and Karma through *Māyā* and love."

Oh yeah, this sounds perfect. I can just imagine going back to the hotel and telling the wife that according to the *Gītā*, sweet lips, you are my greatest enemy, as because of you I am being lured deeper into the abyss of karmic bondage. Wow. That ought to be fun and mainly unprintable.

"But the reality of one's situation is that, you or I cannot just leave our loved ones. And also we do not advocate people leaving their homes just in order to avoid being further enticed into the karmic cycle. What we advocate is that staying where you are, transform or change people who are in your orbit. So first and foremost you start with yourself, change yourself and then change your home scenario and transform it. Bring in the Image of Light or the Light Body also called your subtle self you must send vibrations of peace and tranquillity to people at home, the work place, in your friend circle, gymnasium, wherever you feel there is somebody who is first bringing out the worst in you or really shaking your core of equilibrium. There are negative people or souls, who surround you, and the first step is to start sending them vibrations of peace. Visualize rays of light, filled with peace and positivity emitting from you entering the person, and this can be done only when you are in the image of the soul, when you are completely centered. Let the ray's envelope those who are negative and hateful and pray for peace and chant *Ṣanti* or *Peace*. Earlier, when I used to attend office, some colleagues through their actions or words would make me either angry or negative towards them. We waste the maximum energy through stress and anger. So before you start trying to bring peace and joy to all of creation, you need to start working on those closest to you.

"Remember when you want to grow spiritually you have to be completely unattached to all and especially the results of your actions or your efforts, be it in relationships or work. Now, while in meditation using the *Buđhi* or mind and intellect if I happen to remember anyone, though not deliberately, then too I find obstructions in my spiritual work. Spiritual work is done in great speed or *Gati* and within the confines of the *Kāḷ Chakra* or the wheel of time. This movement of time, requires complete centeredness of your being and the more *Gati* or speed that you wish it to move ahead, the more silence needs to be within you. All growth and spiritual work can only take place when you are filled with an incessantly increasing *Ākāś Tatva* or the element of silence. Scientists are also thinking about the co-relation between time, space and speed. Everything has emerged from the *Ākāś Tatva* and one needs to be filled with silence to really perform to one's greatest capabilities.

"Now, when the *Ātmā*, in its subtle form goes up... and when will the *Ātmā* go up in its subtle form to the *Ākāś Tatva* to gain energy... only when it is in the state of desirelessness. That is why when somebody dies and if there are desires or *Moh*, then the subtle body remains confined to the gravity of the earth, and the soul will roam about on earth as per its desires and karmic account. What can one do if one has committed very heavy Karmas?

Alive or dead, the subtle body would become discharged and one gets earth bound. This rule applies to even the *Devis* and *Devatās*.

"A 100-Trillion *Šivas* make one *Māhā Šiva* and that is why though every month a *Śivarātri* comes about, a *Māhā Śivarātri* is celebrated once a year. *Śivarātri* is the limited finite while *Māhā Śivarātri* is the unlimited force. A 100-Trillion *Sūryas* or suns, equal to One *Māhā Sūrya*. Now even inside the *Māhā Sūrya* there is a black hole. When does a black hole come into being? *Māhā Śiva* is in the *Māhā Sūrya*, and inside the *Māhā Sūrya*, *Māhā Śiva* and *Māhā Śakti* created *Sṛuśti* through the power of the *Paṛam Tatvas*. This *Sṛuśti* carried on till the power of the *Paṛam Tatvas* got depleted due to *Sañkalps*. The *Paṛam Tatva* got depleted and that's when *Māhā Sūrya* became *Māhā Kāḷ Agni* which is called the Black Hole. It can devour within itself countless galaxies or *Anant Koti Brāhṁāñḍs* within seconds. Now that became negative as it has taken into it the 'negative'. *Māhā Śiva* then goes to the Absolute Authority to take power. If the Creator gets power, then His creations and their creations will get powers.

"Similarly when an individual's causal and astral body needs power and it doesn't know how to get that power, the soul then becomes negative. If it becomes negative then what will it do? Then it becomes earth bound. For the Demi Gods, one day corresponds to one year on earth. Why? Because the world up there is made of three elements and there is less heaviness in the three elements. The gross world is heavy due to it being made-up of five elements. Where there is heaviness, time moves very slowly. And so in the five elements, where there is pain, we experience it as an ocean of sadness and pain; so when we are sad or in pain it seems eternity and when there is joy, time moves swiftly." Bapuji looked around and then continued.

"The 1st *Lok* or world dimension is in reality our physical world on earth. (I shall call *Lok* or world, as 'dimension', as this is what I have been taught.) *Bhu* means *Dhàṛti* or Earth. When we say we are residing on *Bhu*, it means we are residing on *Mrutyu Lok* or the land of the dead or where death takes place.

"The second world is the *Bhubhrū Lok*. In that there are three-elemental souls. There are *Dharṁ Pitās* or various Heads of religion sitting and it is the subtle world. There are some exceptionally wonderful souls here and they wish to do very noble work and go to the 3rd *Lok* or world or dimension that is the *Swarg Lok* or heaven. So, to go to *Swarg Lok*, they need to become completely desire-less. In the second *Lok* though they have three-elemental bodies the *Ākāś* element is less. That is why focus on becoming without any desires or *Nih-Sañkalp* and gain more *Ākāś Tatva* and move on to the next *Lok*.

"The Heaven as we know it is in the 3rd World or *Lok* or Dimension. In the 3rd *Lok* or *Swarg Lok* or 3rd Dimension, the amount of *Ākāś Tatva* is high. That is the reason why using *Sañkalps* one can get what one wants in that Dimension. The 3rd Dimension also has the Tree of Manifestations called the *Kalp Vruksh* that can manifest and give everything that one wants. Thirty-three crore *Devatās* or Gods and Goddesses of this *Brähṁāñḍ* were staying there.

"Then above the *Swarg Lok*, are the 4th and the 5th *Loks*. In the 4th *Lok*, in one day of *Brähṁā* time, all the earlier 3 *Loks* get destroyed; even the *Devatās* get destroyed. So all three *Loks, Bhu, Bhubhrū* and *Sva* or *Swarg Lok* get destroyed and that is called *Kalp Prälai*.

"So when the *Devatās* get a cue that all the three *Loks* are going to be destroyed, the ones that are *Satya Pradhān Devatās* or those Demi Gods who are filled with truth and without any desire, they go to the 4th and the 5th *Lok*. So when we go to the 4th and the 5th *Lok*, up there, there is a complete silence zone. There is absolute silence. Over here differentiation of male and female disappears and the Soul Image or *Ātmā Swarūp* increases and strengthens.

"Thus, in the 3rd *Lok,* called the *Swarg Lok* there are three ways in which you spend time. One is through *Sañkalps* or intentions. Whatever you desire you can materialize but if the *Sañkalp* is made through the soul then the energy is wasted, so the individual would come back to earth. There are those who have the knowledge and know that they have to go beyond all this. So slowly all their actions and thoughts and words move towards being desire-less and selfless. They begin to become *Nih-Sañkalp.* By being in the state of *Nih-Sañkalp*, the level of *Ākāś Tatva* increases in their body. If the level of *Ākāś Tatva* increases in the body, depending on this increase in the *Ākāś Tatva*, the soul would go to the 4th, the 5th the 6th *Loks* and then reach *Brähṁāpuri.*

"Now even after going into *Brähṁāpuri,* there is the risk of pride. The soul has become like *Brähṁā.* The soul can materialize anything it desires. The chances of *Ahañkār* or pride with the knowledge that *'I have become Brähṁā',* is immense. Thus, even in *Brähṁāpuri* there are stages or layers but basically in this place, you have as much *Śakti* or energy as *Brähṁā,* to create whatever you may desire."

Now back to my two bit. So basically the higher the dimension you rise to, the more the power you have, and with greater power the chances of one getting sucked into subtle attachment of *Māyā* increases tremendously. Imagine if one realizes that he or she can create galaxies and begin a civilization with just a thought, the chances of materializing different worlds and civilizations must be alluringly powerful. To be able to start or create a civilization which contains all that you yearned for and basically become the God of that creation. You would want it to be the ideal place for one and all, or a one, big, night-life spot, whatever it may be the temptation to become a creator or a Demi God, must be really alluring. The more you get caught up in that power, means eventually you come back to earth due to all the *Sañkalps* or intentions you have materialized when in the *Loks*. So the higher one rises, the wider the net spreads for one to be caught up in *Māyā* and the karmic abyss. I assume our Creator really yearns only for those who want nothing else but to be with Him. The less you are caught up with yourself, the higher you shall rise. But the higher you rise there are more subtle ways of getting caught up with the ego and yourself.

According to me if you want to reach the Beyond of the Beyond you have to go Beyond the Beyond of Yourself. The individual self is the greatest hurdle to cross. Once you go beyond yourself then and only then will one merge in the Beyond of the Beyond and merge with our extremely elusive, playing hard-to-get Creator.

Thus, in short, to briefly encapsulate all this business of merging with the Creator, at least I am going to be spending a really long, long time on planet earth.

"Betā," continued *Bapuji*, "a person's destination after he or she leaves the body, depends not only on one's Karma in this life time but his *Sanchit* Karmas or collective Karmas of various births that the soul has a recording of. This recording is in the causal body of each individual. Remember each individual first has to travel 84-lakhs *Yonis* before gaining human birth."

Yoni means a womb and it is believed that one has to go through 84-lakh wombs – basically there are 84-lakh different species – before one is born as a human being. Looking at us, human beings, and the way we are going about disrespecting life and all of creation, I wonder why the fuss about becoming a human being. The specie called human being is largely overrated in the cosmic evolution chart. Back to *Bapuji*.

"After 84-lakh births in different species, we get the

human soul, to do good work, through which then we can commence our journey to *Swarg Lok* or heaven. To go to *Swarg Lok,* one needs to be a human. What happens to the soul? *Ātmā* is *Amar Avinashi,* it is immortal. Through the accounts of one's Karmas, one's speed is determined. If the individual has done good Karma, then there is *Satya Gati* or Godspeed. It means the soul goes upward. And *Dur Gati* is when the soul goes down. And a soul whose entire focus is on his or her family, or life on earth, remains earth bound. Remember the saying, *'Ant Mati So Gati',* which means that at the time of death, when the soul leaves the body, the final thoughts, mood, inclination present in the *Buđhi* or mind of a person decides the *Gati* or movement, speed and direction of the soul. If the individual is not attached to the family, then the *Buđhi* or higher mind will be attached to something else. So let us assume the soul goes to his Guru. Where is the Guru residing? In the second world which is called the *Bhubhrū Lok*. In that there are three-elemental souls. There are *Dharṁ Pitā's* or heads of religion sitting and it is the subtle world.

"*Bhubhrū Lok,* is a place where three-elemental souls and all *Dharṁ* Gurus reside. Over here too there are many *Māhā Ruśimunis* sitting, along with Gurus, and they say that if you want to move higher then you have to go through the Gurus who will further guide you on your soul's journey. Every star has its own world. So where was *Śani Maharaj* or Saturn living… in *Śani Lok*. So who made *Śani*…the planet? Lord *Śani* Himself. Lord *Śukra* or Venus made *Śukra Lok*. Why were these planets made? They were made so that their creations could stay there in the three-elemental framework. Thirty-three crore Demi Gods and Goddess have made their own worlds for their creations to inhabit.

"All great souls, pure souls, who wish for good work to be done, live in *Bhubhrū Lok* with the main purpose to guide those souls that come up to move further upwards. It is from here that *Sañchālan* or management of earth takes place. When an individual drops his or her body and through karmic actions finds itself in this *Lok*, then the soul is guided and helped to move further upwards. The Masters leave the final choice of where the individual wants to move up to the individual. Free will is very important in all the worlds. If you want to move upwards so be it. You want to be reborn for whatever reason so be it. Now let us say you want to be reborn once again as a human being, but your power seems to be less to turn into a human, so then the Masters will teach you certain *Tapasyās* or spiritual exercises or penance, to fill your soul with power, so that you can become a human again."

"And what about earthbound souls?" I inquired.

"I had seen on Discovery channel or maybe some other channel, but I think it was the Discovery channel, where a man dies and he did not want his daughter to marry a particular man. After his death, his daughter marries the same man of her choice. So the father enters his son-in-law and troubles his own daughter repeatedly till the marriage breaks. Earlier those in the West did not believe in three-elemental beings or spirits or ghosts… now due to advancement in technology they have captured on film and tape, photographs and recordings, to show that spirits abound and are near their loved ones. In our land of India, we believe in the *Pitru Lok* or the Abode of Ancestors. Most religions perform the death ceremony and have other rituals for the departed.

"The Hindus believe and perform prayers and a ceremony for the departed called the *Pitru Tarpan*. So when the *Pitru Tarpan* takes place, what is the meaning of that? For *Pitru Tarpan*, we go to *Gāyā*, *Kāshi*, on the banks of *Narmadā*, or *Trimbakeshwar* or *Subhramanyā* among other places. Why are these places recommended? That is because these places are meeting grounds of all those spirits who want to move forward but need a bit of help. The prayers bring about a vibrational change and give knowledge to the spirits and help them to move forward. So the three-elemental souls take *Jñān* or knowledge and then those really desirous of moving-on ascend towards other *Loks*."

"Is there a designated place called the *Pitru Lok* or a dimension for ancestors?" I inquired.

"Long time back it was on the moon."

"And why have they shifted residence and to where?"

"Now they can stay wherever they want. Their residential place is up to them and also keeps changing. As time passes, things even in the spirit plane change. Take for example, earlier during our *Pitru Tarpan*, even non-vegetarian food was offered. So for those dead ancestors or *Pitru* who enjoyed non-vegetarian food while on earth, meat and fish were offered during the ceremony. The *Pitru* would enter a family member who was a non-vegetarian, eat through him and go away. This is *Pitru tarpan karna* or giving solace to the souls of our ancestors through an offering of food or *Bhog* and other articles that were dear to them."

"Ok, so apart from taking *Jñān* or knowledge what else takes place in these *Loks*?" I inquired. "What I have understood through various books and now what you are saying is that each *Lok* has numerous stages or layers too. So firstly there are the *Loks* or what we call Dimensions, and within each *Lok* or Dimension, there are different sub-dimensions or sub-stages or layers which depict the growth of each individual. Those from the higher Dimensions can visit the lower ones since they have more power and soul strength, but through that power and soul strength, the danger of getting sucked again in *Māyā* and *Sañkalp*s is very much present."

"Yes *betā*. Very true and this is how it works. When a person dies, the soul reaches its destination, depending upon accumulated Karma of this life and all lives ever lived. When the soul becomes aware it needs to move upwards and yet not get sucked into the business of *Sañkalps*, the soul becomes *Naśto Mohā* or lighter and devoid of attachments and desires, and resultant the gravitational pull reduces and thus the *Ākāś Tatva* increases paving way for the soul to move further upwards. In the *Bhubhrū Lok* where Masters, Sages and really top-quality souls reside, there are four types of layers. First of all when one goes up there, it reaches the first layer and one can see friends and family and loved ones from above and there is longing and craving to be part of them. It is natural to feel like being amongst your lot. Thoughts and emotions engulf the individual here too. That is the power of *Māyā*. Thoughts of guilt enter too. 'I have left them and come, I should not have come, I should have stayed down and helped, I would have helped them in the three elements and I would do this and that', so the soul *Tadapti Hai* or suffers a bit. Sometimes the soul may not be able to handle this and go down in three elements to be near his or her loved ones and to help them. Often the soul then gets stuck and becomes earthbound. Many times soul journeys are taken up and down, though the soul resides mainly up. But as those on earth forget their loved ones or don't need them as acutely as before or feel that they aren't needed as much as earlier; the soul realizes that it needs to move-on with its journey too. This could take a short time or a really long time. All depends on what the soul really craves for.

"In the first layer of the 2nd *Lok,* there are *Ruśis* residing but They let the soul or individual workout his or her *Māyā* or illusion of attachments. They let the person suffer as it is the personal choice of the soul to suffer by being still caught-up with relationships and personal ego. So They let the soul suffer as with suffering, the soul's *Manomayē Vikās*, spiritual cleansing and progress takes place and all *Vikār* or decay due to bad Karmas or sins of the *Mun* or heart are cleared with this suffering.

"Then, with the realization that it needs to continue with its journey, the soul moves up to the next layer of the 2nd *Lok*. In the second layer Sages give appropriate guidance and true knowledge. The *Māhā Ruśis* give you the choice to decide 'where do you want to go from here? Do you want to go still higher?' So if the soul wants to ascend They teach the soul the ritual and give it the knowledge to move upwards."

"So the soul is taught certain spiritual exercises, devotion and meditation or *Sadhana* that helps the soul to move upwards?"

"Yes *betā*. So then the soul goes into *Sadhana*. So what is this *Sadhana*? It is to become in the Image of the Soul. Image of the Soul as in the *Ākāś* element in it increases and then it travels to the third layer. So the soul moves to the third layer where the Sages seated in meditation are more powerful and spiritually advanced than the ones seated in the second layer. They are with still higher and better quality soul power. So They make the individual want to move up higher. So they guide the individual and give more knowledge and methods of going to the fourth layer. In the fourth layer the *Dharṁ* Gurus or the Founding Fathers of all religions and Perfect Masters reside.

"Remember this 4th stage of the 2nd dimension, as you call it, is very important for the soul as once these layers are transcended the soul can really take a massive leap into the land of the Gods; *Brāhṁāpuri, Viśnupuri* and *Param Dhām* and the Absolute Authority. So in the fourth stage of the *Lok* there are Masters of all religious beliefs, all *Dharam Pitās* are sitting separately. And with the *Dharṁ Pitās* there are very many *Ātmās*."

So basically forget everything but one thing, if you want to move upwards, go beyond the self. That's the be all and end all of all liberation.

I have a difference of opinion with *Bapuji* on a serious issue. Often he would say that the Masters sit in the 2nd *Lok* or Dimension and never come down and the role of Their followers is to gain more followers. *Bābā Sai* too cannot come down or get too involved with His children down here, as if He does, their pull will drag Him down and He too will be caught up in the five-elemental pull. *Bapuji* also believes that whoever have their temples and other religious places of worship cannot move higher, till all those idols etc. are destroyed as Their subtle ego is tied up with Their devotees.

My take is different. I feel the Masters are on that level in the spirit plane, as the 2nd *Lok,* is the crucial Dimension, as it is in this Dimension that the soul is really getting prepared to become selfless and work only for the good of all creation. It is in this stage that the soul can either get all entangled in *Māyā* and its forces, those of the loved ones on Earth, or get mesmerized with the beauty and power of the spirit plane. Also at this level, the souls who have gathered near their Masters are already on a substantially high level of growth, and they can help followers of the Master who still are either in the lower Dimensions or on earth. Yes, the Master will not come down. He or She doesn't need to. *The Army of Light Workers* work as *Guides and Guardian Angels* and of course there are *Archangels and Angels*, who are always there for all those who call out to Them. The Master allows His Energy to be channelled and guidance given, either directly or through a medium and channel. The message will reach the child through a medium who could be a psychic or through a billboard hoarding. The Master's ways are mysterious and real. For the Master to come down and grace a disciple, the child's love should be all encompassing and faith all pervading. *Bābā Sai* of *Shirdi,* often through channelling, has mentioned that *"Shraḍha Itni Honi Chahiye Ke Guru Ko Hila Dey"* – "One's faith in one's Guru should be so strong and pure that it shakes the very Guru".

So if your love and faith is truly selfless and you can shake your Master with your faith, patience, love for your Master, then I know that your Master will come down for you. He has to come down for you. Just don't get mathematical with your Master. Don't put conditions. Don't try to blackmail Him. Just love Him. Truly love Him and then when you call out to Him, trust me, He will come. Let me give you an example. Let us say you love somebody truly and that person loves you truly too. Let us assume you love your child and your child can't do without you, loves you unconditionally. Imagine if your child were in some sort of trouble. Wherever you are, and if your child were to call out to you, wouldn't you leave everything and be there for your child? Whether you were in the physical plane or one of the various *Loks,* if your child was in real need and called out to you with all his or her love, wouldn't you reach your child? I would. I am sure you would too. Now a Master has within His or Her soul, maternal and paternal love which is deeper than the deepest ocean, wider than creation and as giving as Mother Earth. Then why wouldn't your Master not be with you?

Also can you imagine the love the Masters, *Rūśimunis* or Sages and *Dharṁ Pitās* or religious heads, have for either their followers or just one and all, that instead of moving and merging with the Creator or The Absolute Authority (and They can easily do so, as They are beyond the self and are filled with realization of Oneness with the Creator), They still remain in the 2nd *Lok* or dimension, just to guide others to move forward and grow spiritually and progress to the above dimensions? Can you imagine the love They must feel for all of creation, to not merge with the Lord, but stay behind to guide others?

If this isn't humbling, and if this doesn't urge one to make the Master happy and proud and try one's level best to spread love, peace, happiness, compassion, joy to those around us and to those in need of help and compassion, then spiritually there is nothing else that is going to light your bulb. Unless you are one of those who just wants liberation for yourself. Good luck with that.

10

So next morning after appeasing *Meher* with a really cool gift, which in reality was just the shower cap provided by the Hotel, I entered *Bapuji's Āśrăm*. It was a Thursday, a day I abstained from smoking and I had a day of channelling after the interviews. It was a foggy day. The car's fog beams were switched on, at ten-thirty in the morning. What a city!

"So, now we move to the 3rd *Lok.*" I began the interview. I was once again huddled on *Bapuji's* bed, with two blankets covering me.

"*Swarg Lok.* Who goes into the *Swarg Lok*? This *Lok* is of different qualities. In each and every *Lok* there are four layers or stages. Initially, when one enters the third *Lok*, in the first stage, there is no regalia and luxuries nor much happiness and conveniences. And this is done on purpose to make the soul move higher to the 2nd and 3rd and it is only in the 4th stage of *Swarg Lok* that there is opulence and luxuries, etc. which is called *Bhog Vilās*. *Bhog Vilās* is the power to relish and gratify in the three elements, as there is the *Kalp Vruksh*."

"Now what is the *Kalp Vruksh*?" I was getting giddy with all these *Sanskrit* words. They always used fancy words for everything. It would be interesting to see those chaps from the days yonder verbally fight each other. "Good sir of a deflowered tramp, you entered the five-elemental world before thy mother obtained a certificate for legalizing fornication."

"The *Kalp Vruksh* is a tree. It was during the time of

Sāgar Manthan that the *Kalp Vruksh* had emerged. It can grant all wishes. Lord *Indra* was the one to take it to *Swarg*. Like we have trees here, similarly there are trees there too but made of different elements. For instance, the Holy Ganges too was in the astral world till it was brought down through Lord *Śiva*.

"So, the Ganges was not made of the element of water. It was a vibration feel of flowing water, something that cannot be described but has to be seen. But those days the Ganges had super power. It contained the elements of *Vāyu* and *Agni* or Air and Fire. Water runs on the combination of the elements of *Vāyu* and *Agni*. So in this level of *Swarg Lok* pleasures galore abide. One can lose oneself in the pleasures of three-elemental drink, food and bodily pleasures."

Bodily pleasures without the body; wow, that must be really hard core erotica. For a while I truly tried to ponder about all the spirits having a wicked night-out but for the life of me couldn't understand how anybody could go wild about bodily pleasures when the three-elemental Casanova didn't have a blasted body but was in reality, made up of Ether, Air and Fire.

"Drink, food and sex, that's a good joint to be in, say what *Bapuji*." *Bapuji* began to laugh loudly.

"They indulge in lots of pleasure and of course that is where the danger lies. You can get consumed by the pleasures offered in this level of *Swarg Lok*. Whatever pleasures one seeks is available. Name it. Think it. It materializes. Very dangerous place to be in *betā*, as eventually all that a human being may have desired is his or her for the asking."

"But there may be some nut-case souls who aren't interested in all this too?" There's no telling about souls, I tell you.

"Oh yes, there are souls who can see through the

entrapment. They may warn other souls, but you know how it is. The logic is 'let me enjoy this for a while and then I will continue with my spiritual journey'."

So I guess after having the mother of all parties, the soul exhausts all its good accumulated Karmas and then the poor sod of a soul has run-out of fuel to move upwards and the laws of karmic gravity pull the soul back down to the five elements, to work out his or her other Karmas.

"But there are souls who can see through the entrapment of pleasures offered in *Swarg Lok* or are just not interested in all this or who manage to get out of the entrapment of supreme pleasures quickly and then the soul will move onwards to the 4th *Lok*, which is called the *Māhā Lok*.

"In *Māhā Lok*, there is one *Anś* or speck of the *Māhā Tatva*. There is a presence of the *Māhā Tatva* or the Great Element, so the one who lives in the vibrations of the *Māhā Tatva* or the Great Element, that person has no desires of any sort any more. There is supreme Silence in the *Māhā Tatva;* infact the meaning of *Māhā Tatva* is Supreme Silence.

"If the *Māhā Tatva* is a super computer, the other *Tatvas* are like the old fashioned type-writers; this is the kind of difference between *Māhā Tatva* and other *Tatvas*. One could say it is a very refined form of the *Ākāś Tatva*. The *Ākāś Tatva* emerged from the *Māhā Tatva*. After going into the *Māhā Tatva*, a lot of power comes into the soul. There too *Māhā Ruśis* reside, giving suggestions and help to other people or souls on how to go beyond the *4th Lok* to the next level above. The Sages give knowledge and show more subtle ways of moving ahead."

Remember these *Māhā Ruśis* have sacrificed Their own growth in order to serve all of creation, by helping and encouraging other souls to move on.

"Are there stages in the *4th Lok* or Dimension too?"

"In every *Lok* or Dimension there are layers or stages.

Just know that there are four stages in each *Lok* or World or Dimension."

"So what do the souls do in the 4th *Lok* or *Māhā Lok*?"

"Son, the ego is so dense and vast and accumulated that it takes slow and continuous, refined cleansing, to get rid of it. And remember, at each step one needs to be careful, as the ego can raise its head, anytime and anywhere. The focus is to keep moving ahead but one needs to be careful of the ego and subtle desires. The focus of all souls in this *Lok* is to reach *Brāhṁāpuri*. The Sages help each and every one to keep progressing."

"So now from *Māhā Lok*, we come to the 5th *Lok*, and it is called the *Jan Lok*...? Now what happens in this 5th Dimension?"

"Yes. In *Jan Lok*, there is a deeper state of silence and joy. And there is such divine music playing that in fact it helps in gaining deeper and deeper levels of silence and virtually all desires are washed away. The 6th Dimension is *Tap Lok*. In *Tap Lok*, the souls perform *Tapasyā* or *Tap* in short, to reach *Brāhṁāpuri*."

"What *Tapasyā* do they do? And why, as they seem to be sort of cleansed away of all desires?"

"*Tapasyā* or spiritual rituals and penance to clean away even an *Anś* or the minutest speck of rage and anger or pride from your soul. So, even if there is a slight speck of anger or rage or pride or ego left still, that would mean the soul still has rubbish in it and through this ritual or rite, even if there is a speck of *Vikarm* or residue of negative Karma, with the performance of the *Tapasyā*, these remnant specks of ego get burnt away to further purify the soul. And most importantly, at the same time, the level of *Ākāś Taŧva* is increased substantially. With the increase in the *Ākāś Taŧva* the soul immediately moves ahead and enters *Brāhṁāpuri*."

This is the 7th *Lok*. This is the 7th Dimension. This is the 7th Heaven. Welcome to *Brähṁāpuri*.

"One second in *Brähṁāpuri* or the land of *Brähṁā*, equals to one-lakh years on Earth. Just like one moment or one second of *Māhā Śiva* equals to *Brähṁā's* 100 years. So, in our galaxy or in our *Brähṁāñḍ* one second is equal to one-lakh years on Earth. So if you stay for one day in *Brähṁāpuri* and come back to earth, eight-trillion sixty-four-crore years on earth will have passed. And we have not yet spoken of *Viśnupuri* time which moves much faster and then above that is *Śivpuri* and still above that is *Paṛam Dhām*. This calculation of time belongs only to our *Brähṁāñḍ* or galaxy or world. If we go down to *Pātāl Lok* or hell then the time there moves much, much slower than on *Bhu Lok* or Earth.

"As the name suggests, this place is inhabited by Lord *Brähṁā*. So whichever soul reaches *Brähṁāpuri* that soul becomes like *Brähṁā*. Even if the One Up There, comes on Earth in the form of a human being, He too becomes a human being and then all the rules that apply to the five elements will apply to Him as well. In the same way, all souls that reach *Brähṁāpuri* become like *Brähṁā* and have the power to create like *Brähṁā*. But They do not remain for long in *Brähṁāpuri* as who does *Brähṁā* relentlessly remember? He remembers Lord *Viśnu*. For it is from the navel of Lord *Viśnu* that Lord *Brähṁā* has emerged. Navel means *Śakti* or power. Lord *Brähṁā* continuously takes direction from Lord *Viśnu*.

"And the 8th *Lok* or World or Dimension is *Viśnupuri*… the Creator of Lord *Viśnu* is *ŚivaŚakti* in the *Rūp* of *ArdhNāreśwar*. *ArdhNāreśwar* is Lord *Śiva* and *Mā Pārvati* merged as one; half is Lord *Śiva* and the other half is *Mā Pārvati* or *Mā Śakti*. Thus *ŚivaŚakti* is above *Viśnupuri*. Earlier, till *Brähṁāpuri* even the *Asurs* or the Demons would reach after doing *Tapasyā* or spiritual penance to gain special privileges or blessings called *Vardāns* from Lord *Brähṁā*. They would reach *Brähṁāpuri;* but *Viśnupuri* not all would be able to reach. Only the *Devatās* or Demi Gods and Goddesses would be able to reach and go to *Viśnupuri*.

"But reaching *Śivpuri*, which is the 9th *Lok* or World or Dimension is not an easy feat. Even Lord *Viśnu* would not be able to go to *Śivpuri*. So, what did Lord *Śiva* do? He sent one of His cells as Lord *Shañkar* on earth, in the Himalayas and sent the message down that; 'those who want to talk to Me, talk to Lord *Shañkar*. Lord *Shañkar* will communicate back to Me.' Thus, even *Shañkar* always remembers *Śiva* or Himself.

"The 10th *Lok* is above *Śivpuri* which is *Paṛam, Paṛam Dhām* where only *Ātmā Nirākāri* or only those souls who are completely without an atom of the self or desires, exist."

The final destination, according to me is even beyond the 10th dimension. The final frontier is in reality the 11th dimension. Here one merges with the Absolute Authority, becoming Him-Her. That is why *Bābā Sai of Shirdi* keeps telling one and all in channeling that there are eleven main chakras. The eleventh chakra is the 11th Dimension.

11

I was back in the *Āśrăm*. *Mataji* was with me. We shared a cup of tea and began to converse.

"If you *Nāth* something what does it mean? It means to control that thing. So what is *Bapuji's* role? He is *Amarnāth* – the one to control the *Amar* or Eternal Element. Only a truly knowledgeable one can teach the spiritual child or seeker how to *Nāth* or control the *Amar* Element. Which children will receive this eternal element? The ones who selflessly love as only in selfless love is true power. The ones who love will be given the power. Now come we will go to *Bapuji*. He waits for you every morning enthusiastically, like a lost friend."

We enter *Bapuji's* room and he greets me warmly. I touch his feet and he blesses me and then makes sure I am covered properly with a thick blanket. We both have our heads covered with skull caps. *Mataji* seems to be fine with just a shawl. I have no idea why women are called the weaker sex… or for that matter the better half…

"*Bapuji* now that we are done with various stages of heaven, let's go downwards into the bowels of hell." I might as well get to know the layout and the roadmap of the other side; just in case.

"Now which *Ātmās* are there in *Pātāl Lok*? *Pātāl Lok* means under the *Dhàṛti* or Earth."

"When you say under the earth, do you really mean our Earth?"

"Many people think it is under the earth, miles and

miles below our very earth's surface. But in reality it is like another planet under our revolving planet Earth. Absolutely down below in the three-elemental stage. Just like the moon and the sun are above earth, *Pātāl Lok* or hell is below Mother Earth. *Śāstras* or our religious books say that hell is ten-thousand *Yojan* below our planet. Now we know what a mile or a kilometer stands for, but none of us really know what a *Yojan* indicates. It is an old metric system of measuring distance, but no one really knows how many miles or kilometers a *Yojan* truly stands for. Thus in our *Śāstras,* they have bluffed a little bit. They say that it is inside the Earth but there is nothing inside the Earth but lava. So, below our earth at a distance of 10 thousand *Yojans,* is *Pātāl Lok.*

"The *Nirākār Śiva* is the formless Creator. *Nirākār Śiva* thought that 'I should become Many from One'. So from *Śiva Nirākāri,* the formless One, came *Śiva Ākāri,* the One with form, and *ŚivaŚakti* was created. From Lord *Śiva* came about Lord *Viśnu* and from Lord *Viśnu's* navel, Lord *Brāhṁā* emerged. Then Lord *Brāhṁā* through his *Sañkalps* or intentions made the *Sapt Ruśis* or the seven *Mānas Putras* or mind-born sons of *Brāhṁā* represented as the Archer in the sky. The seven *Ruśis* made the Seven *Lok*'s or Dimensions. After the seven *Ruśis,* the *Manuśya Lok* or human world was made. After *Manuśya Lok* or the human world, the *Manuśya Ātmā* or human soul was created, the first of the lot being *Manu* and *Satarupa.* Now remember we are talking about our galaxy created by our *Śiva, Viśnu* and *Brāhṁā.* This way there are trillions of galaxies. Our creators come from the 108 who come from the Absolute Authority. Now trillions of galaxies like ours are made and destroyed. We need to move beyond the finite and into the infinite. Focus on the Absolute Authority; The true Creator of the Infinite, who has no name, *Rūp* or form, *Rang* or colour; nothing. He always was, is and will always remain. So the creator of our *Brāhṁāñḍ* or galaxy is *Śiva.* But the one who has a name is not the Almighty Authority. The Almighty Authority is without name, form or colour."

Ok, let us get everything into perspective. Earth is part of our solar system which has the sun and everything is contained by the gravity of the sun. So we have the sun, major planets, small planets, the asteroids, the Kuiper belt objects, comets, meteoroids and interplanetary dust. *The Milky Way* is the name of our galaxy and our galaxy alone has at least 100 to 400 billion stars!

Scientists and astronomers are of the opinion that there could be more than about five hundred billion galaxies in the universe. In fact the most recently discovered "Phoenix" system the largest galaxy yet, touted to be 6-billion years old creates about 740 stars a year. So multiply that by 6 billion years.... Thus that galaxy may contain more than tens and thousands of trillions of stars. Our very own *Milky Way* measures 100,000 light years distance and ours is one of the smallest galaxies in the universe. Our galaxy is like a small pepper seed in proportion to the size of the universe. Remember scientists are even now contemplating that even beyond the one hundred billion galaxies that make up our universe, there is a distinct possibility that there may be many universes beyond ours.

Ok, now we come to what goes on in hell? For some reason, *Bapuji* wasn't too keen on this aspect and summarized it quickly. This is basically what came through. The first stage is called *Atal Lok* or Pig-headed or Rigid Land. When the soul comes down to earth, it has the choice of doing good or bad, getting entangled further in *Māyā* and karmic bondage or soaring towards the Light, and either trying to become selfless or selfish and most importantly, becoming attached either to the spirit or to the body. In this *Lok*, just like we have a human body, there though it is a body of three elements, the body feels far heavier as all the elements are very dense. Time moves very slowly here. One day could seem like decades on earth. The body is a combination of many varying *Tatvas*. The set up is very similar to that of Earth. All that you have been caught-up with on earth multiply it by a few hundred times and that is what goes on there. Basically after talking with *Bapuji* what I could decipher was that down below, it is very much like Earth and everything is present but there is no peace in the heart or taste on the tongue; no joy or happiness and no sense of peace and composure. So you may have everything down there but you do not have the power to enjoy anything. All that which an individual has yearned for or lusted for is given to him but it brings no joy or happiness; everything is tasteless, senseless, making everything a thousand-times more frustrating. Imagine if you are thirsty and you drink water and your thirst still never gets quenched. You try water, some juice, beer, whatever you can think of which would normally quench your thirst, and the more you consume, you only get thirstier.

The Second Dimension of the underworld is very similar to the first one but the vibrations and elements are still more negative and heavier, so one basically gets further fried in the brain and kicked between the legs. The person begins to get more frustrated, restless, uneasy and anxious. Life is very similar to what it is on earth. Whatever you have desired you still may get but there is no sense of gratification. Imagine a state of perpetual unease. As *Bābā Sai of Shirdi* so often says, heaven and hell are a state of mind.

Then if you have rogered even further when back on earth, then you go to the third Dimension of hell, where the elements are still heavier than the first two, and time passes so slowly that one gets breathless and suffocated just by the seemingly stillness of time. I think the worst part of it all, is that you may still have all what you have wanted or lusted for but you just can't quench your thirst, satiate your appetite and time just doesn't seem to pass.

According to *Bapuji* what makes it worse is that people over there are in a constant state of frustration, conflict and in anger, thus making one and all cruel, violent and filled with hate. As you go further below, the very vibration is filled with hate, anger and restlessness. Each one is filled with thoughts of how to torture the other and make life more miserable and be able to rule over the other; and thus violence and unheard of physical, mental and emotional anguish is perpetuated, by those who have more power or by those who have ganged up around you. As further you sink, time ceases to virtually pass; more intense restlessness, anger, frustration, hate, guilt, and the inability to enjoy anything, even if you have everything; each moment becomes unbearable, till the soul decides, enough is enough, and I want to move ahead. The moving ahead is painfully slow. The growth of the individual will depend on his or her desire to be set free from one's baser instincts and to serve all of creation. Remember, the individual has everything going against him or her. You are in an environment that is dense and volatile; time doesn't seem to pass, and you now want to move upwards. The journey will depend on which stage of digression you are in and the lower the dimension, the harder it is to move upwards, as one needs all the patience, all the focus, and the burning desire to be set free. And the more spiritual you become, your guilt assails you all the more; of all the wrong you have done and that could once again detract you, as guilt can cripple the soul as powerfully as anger, hate and greed. So the forces are all against you and if you become against yourself you remain in the bowels of hell till eternity or what would seem like eternity, till your negative Karmas run out and you begin the journey once again back to earth.

"Just like we human beings have to earn everything,

similarly there is great hard work and labour down there. The one in charge of that *Lok* could be cruelness personified; so the stages are *Atal Lok, Vital Lok, Sutal Lok, Talātal Lok, Māhātal Lok* and *Pātāl Lok.* As per the stages of the *Ātamā*, they are sent to these places. There are beings that resemble monsters or *Rākśasas*. They rule. All those who we call *Rākśasas*, like the King of *Pātāl Lok* in reality exist. Basically everything horrible that a human can do happens here and one has to experience it all."

So basically the 7th Dimension of hell, called the *Pātāl Lok,* is the mother of all despair and cruelty. The frustration, agony, sorrow, pain, boredom, and everything one dreads, exists here. Your greatest fears and paranoia's materialize here, but just multiply it by a few hundred times and the worst part of it all is that, time stands still here.

Bapuji also believes that just like up there in heaven, there are further stages beyond the 7th Dimension; just like when the soul is moving upwards, becoming more selfless, it moves beyond the 7th Dimension, to *Brāhṁāpuri* then *Viśnupuri* and then *Śivpuri*, even in what we call hell, there are further dimensions below the *Pātāl Lok*; which is the 7th Dimension of the lower world. Those souls who have caused misery to millions of people while on earth; who have inflicted pain, sorrow, distress, to a collective lot of people, through their actions or philosophies or inaction, knowingly or unknowingly caused sorrow, loss, pain, angst to innumerable people; or through violence, destroyed land, homes, families; or through their leadership and orders, their followers pillaged towns and raped women, maimed people, destroyed families and futures; basically brought upon mass scale sorrow and misery, find themselves even below the *Pātāl Lok*.

"Now those who were great sinners while on Earth live even below the *Pātāl Lok* and we believe there are about fifty-five crore such types of hells. So these people live even below the *Pātāl Lok*. The *Māhā* or the worst sinners." *Bapuji* nodded in sadness.

Thus, those who have indulged in mass destruction and been responsible either directly or through his or her ideology or philosophy and dictate, for thousands of people to be killed and innumerable families to suffer untold misery thereafter, find themselves in these places.

My understanding is that the person will experience the pain, sorrow, fear, loss, heartbreak, frustration and all angst experienced, physically, emotionally and mentally, by those who suffered or were killed, directly or indirectly by that individual. And the intensity will be a hundred fold more. Imagine having to undergo the pain, sorrow, misery, doom of each and every person whose life you have taken and the ongoing angst the individual must feel for leaving loved ones behind and watching them suffer; emotionally, mentally, physically and financially. If that isn't hell what is.

"*Ruzbeh*, those who have millions of people killed, are one such category and down below the *Pātāl Lok*, they suffer such punishment that it is indescribable."

Can you imagine the collective grief of millions of people on your soul? I don't believe you are going to be whipped and have the *Agni Tatva* explore various openings in your astral body. I believe hell is just experiencing all the pain you have made others go through, time and again and again, and as the vibrations and elements are so heavy, the pain and misery is multiplied a few hundred times and time just doesn't pass. So once their soul realizes their mistakes, then they move upwards and reach *Pātāl Lok*, which is the 7th Dimension of hell; which when compared to the places below, *Pātāl Lok*, is like a blasted holiday resort. Then after suffering further punishment, they ascend upwards and eventually are born in the human form again. This could take an eternity or feel like an eternity.

"That's a long journey." I mused aloud.

"Yes, remember I told you a soul has to take birth in 84-Lakh *Yonis.* 84-Lakh *Yonis* or Wombs, mean so many different forms or species. This climb from down to top also is included in that. Sinners who have created great misery, have to start right from down, through all the stages of the *Loks* below, then be born in the womb of various species, and then and only then be born as a human, even there, starting from the lowest rung of human evolution. Imagine *betā*, the Lord of 33-crore Gods and Goddesses, Lord *Indra*, He too became a worm in Hell, so say the *Śāstṛās*. Eventually those souls, who were connected with *Indra*, went down into hell and explained to Him and brought him back to *Swarg*."

"You mean somebody who is very spiritually powerful can bring a soul who is languishing in the bowels of hell, back to Earth or Beyond?"

"Yes but that soul from above must be a super *Ātmā* to be able to do so and have the right reasons to do so."

Tie my bollocks in a knot. Influence works there too!!!

"*Nāradmuni* used to reach everywhere saying *Nārāyan....Nārāyan.*"

"So a spiritual power house can go down and work things out?"

"Please understand two things are very important. First, the soul who plans to go down and bring another soul up, needs to be a *Super Ātmā* or else the one who wishes to help too can get stuck in hell. Secondly, the reason for using one's spiritual power to help another soul move upwards quickly must be really valid. A *Satya Prādhan Ātmā* that is the purest of the pure and all God pervasive soul can travel anywhere that soul wishes. If you have a Master and even while in one of the stages of hell you truly are repentant and want to move upwards and your call to your Master is genuine, your Master will hear it and your Master will send His people (*Light Workers*) to help you out. The soul will be given certain spiritual knowledge and through certain spiritual exercises the soul will begin to move upwards at a fast pace. Yes, one has to pay for one's sins and that is then paid out on earth."

So we once again come back to the power of the *Guru* and *Master*, the *Light workers*, the *Archangels* and *Angels*. Their love and importance in our lives is all pervading. Pray more and try to do good. We all are human beings and we shall mess up time and again. All we can do is keep picking ourselves up and keep walking towards Him. He is all Merciful. Approach Him as a child. He is the ultimate personification of maternal love and paternal protection.

Hell and heaven is eventually our own doing. So the logic is simple. Whether you are a *Hindu, Christian, Sikh, Buddhist, Jain, Muslim, Zoroastrian, Native American*, or an agnostic or an atheist, eventually our deeds are going to catch up on us. Good or bad, we are going to experience the intensity a hundred fold greater. Those who believe either just in the Absolute Authority or then in ones Master then the process to move upwards becomes clearer, easier and faster. For those who believe in doing good the path is smooth. For those caught up in ego and all the issues back on earth, the vibrations get dense, the path hazy and the journey upwards more difficult. More you live selflessly the quicker you move up and beyond. You may know of the seven dimensions differently or have other names given to them. But eventually it all is the same. *Brähṁāpuri* may be termed something else, but the fact is that there is life even after the 7th Dimension, which has been mentioned by innumerable Sages and psychics. The name given could be different, but till you don't merge with the One, call Him by any name; Absolute Authority, God, the Creator, *Ahura Mazda, Allah, ŚivaŚakti*, whatever you wish to, the fact of the matter is that the journey continues. We have come from the "Great Flame". We are the sparks from the Great Flame. In us lies dormant all that which the Great Flame embodies. The only real aim of our higher soul is to realize the Oneness of all through the Oneness with "The One". We are going to screw up. That's our inherent birthright. That's ok. We all are in the same boat. Some may be ahead and some behind, but the boat is One and we all are in it. Keep trying to love and go beyond one's small crab-like world. Try to give. It's by giving selflessly you receive His kingdom. Trust me. Try it. Giving is good. Giving is the way one paves one's own path. But don't give with an agenda. Just do. Just give. Just love. Don't try and impress either the Gods or mankind. Don't expect mankind to be grateful. All that you seek, make sure, you seek from the right Source; from your Master and God. Don't judge. Our greatest enemy or critic on earth may be in the spiritual realm our greatest well wisher. Just be. Pray to the One, seeking only blessings to allow you to go through whatever is in store for you calmly, happily, with complete positive surrender and lots of love and to bless you to be able to give your all to life. Ask for joy and love and centeredness even when carrying the cross. Be cool. Have fun. Do whatever it is that lights your bulb, as long as that light shines and dispels darkness, you cannot go wrong. This is what I believe in.

I was back in the hotel. *Meher* was by my side, with her milk bottle in her mouth. I was speaking to somebody on the phone and I guess she heard fragments of what I was speaking. I was tired. After interviewing *Bapuji,* I had gone to a friend, *Anmol's* home, where I had channeled for a couple of hours. I switched off the phone and lay by *Meher*'s side.

"Daddy, why is God only in Heaven?" I sighed. Heaven and hell were a state of mind. We keep making such a blasted song and dance about it. "If He is God, He should be in hell too. How can God *doos* something like that? That is not right. He should be everywhere. What is heaven like Daddy?" She then began to drink milk, seeing Tom and Jerry pillage the house in order to make a point with each other.

"Whenever you think of God, He is there with you love. Heaven, hell, earth, beyond, whenever you think of Him, He has to be with you. If you call out to Him or Her, with all your heart and soul, God has to be with you, no matter where you are. And for me heaven is lying down with you, seeing these ghastly cartoons, hearing the ploch ploch sound of you drinking milk from the bottle and holding you close. That's heaven for me. And when you drive me up the wall, that's hell."

"Sometimes you are very funnies Daddy."

I shut my eyes. Roger the world. I wanted to go to a place where I ceased to exist. God can keep His Heaven and the Demon His Hell. I wanted out; of this whole dance and song, called life; called creation.

The futility of existence never ceases to amaze me.

12

Next day I was back in *Bapuji's* room.

"Now you must understand the Infinite. How have we from the Absolute Authority multiplied into billions of souls. It all began in the *Paṛam Dhām* or the Supreme Abode of the Infinite. The Almighty Authority also thought that He should create a drama or a *natak*."

"Wow. This drama sucks for sure, I hope He knows that."

"If you consider creation as one big drama or *natak*, then you will be greatly entertained."

"Yes I guess so, though life has a tendency of breaking one's heart time and again."

"That is why treat life as one big drama. That's the safest way to go through life. So the Almighty Authority's first creation was The *Paṛam Pitā* or the Founding Father of The Infinite."

This is my interpretation now; Absolute Authority is the producer of the show and the Founding Father, the director and the scriptwriter.

"The creator of the *Paṛam Pitā* is the Almighty Authority. The Founding Father of the Infinite actually began the whole process of creation as we know it. Now certain people might say that *Brähṁā* is the Creator. But the question is who created *Brähṁā*? In reality, the Creator is *Śiva* because *Brähṁā* was created from the navel or energy center of *Viśnu* and *Viśnu* was created by *Śiva*. Thus, *Brähṁā* was not created first, though it was clear that the further role of creation would be in the hands of *Brāhmā*. Thus, we call *Brāhmā* the Creator though even the Creator has another Creator (*Viśnu*) who too has another Creator who is *Śiva*, who too has another creator called the Founding Father of the Infinite who too has another Creator called the Absolute Authority.

"The Almighty Authority is the real Creator and the Founding Father of the Infinite was His first creation and then all of creation was left in the hands of the Founding Father. God is Light. Not this light we are used to. Not the heat of the Sun that burns you in summer. But it was *Paṛam Pṛakāś* or the Supreme Divine Radiance. The Light that always was, is and will be and through this *Paṛam Pṛakāś*, came about the *Māhā Taṫva* which is also Divine Light, but now it is as an element. And then came the *Paṛam, Paṛam, Paṛam Taṫvas* or the Supreme, Supreme, Supreme, elements i.e. *Paṛam Ākāś, Paṛam Vāyu* and *Paṛam Agni*. Then came the *Paṛam Taṫvas* and then just the *Taṫvas*, the five elements."

According to me the Absolute Authority is the combination of *Śiva* and *Śakti,* Supreme Father Energy or God and Supreme Mother Energy or the Goddess, just as proton and electron. The abode is also called *Paṛam Dhām or Paṛam Jyoti* or Supreme Abode or Supreme Divine Radiance. Thus, even the Founding Father of the Infinite is logically the combination of *Śiva and Śakti* energy.

Bapuji and *Sakshi* were a part of this process of explaining things, as often I wouldn't grasp the *Gujarati* or the *Hindi* lingo, *Sakshi* would fill in with the English words.

"So from the Founding Father of the Infinite came the first twelve souls that are worshipped as *Dwadasā Jyotirlingas*. This is represented by the first twelve naturally created *Śivalingas* in this corporeal world! They alone are the ancestors of different religious forefathers! Among them, the first four – two from the left side and two from the right – are the creators of the four elements i.e. Space, Air, Fire and Water. In our *Vedic* scriptures, this place of prime creation is mentioned as *Paṛam Dhām* or Supreme Abode. This is the highest abode, where souls are incorporeal stars of light! Souls remain in their supreme state of being, beyond personality traits, feelings, emotions and actions and are in a complete state devoid of any thoughts and always in a state of bliss. So this *Paṛam Dhām* is the birthplace of the 'Tree of cosmic creation' where souls are in eternal peace and bliss! From the Supreme ball of Power, or *Nebula,* as called by the scientists in the *Big Bang* theory – first emerged twelve souls, then from them another twelve were split which became twenty four souls, which multiplied to 108 souls. These 108 *Paṛam Ātmās* or Supreme Souls were thus first created.

"From the 108 came about 16000 souls. With the creation of the 16000 *Ātmās* the *Paṛam Paṛam Māhā Taŧva* or Divine Light was created. Then from 16000, nine-lakh souls came about. The nine-lakh souls that were created became the seeds of the *Sṛuśti* or creation of the Infinite.

"As these souls were the first ones to come out from the Founding Father of the Infinite or *ŚivaŚakti,* that is why we call them the *Paṛam Ātmās* or Supreme Souls of the Infinite. Over here, the *Vāyu Mandàḷ* or atmosphere started to develop. How did the *Vāyu Mandàḷ* develop? It developed with Divine Light. How did this happen? The *Paṛam Māhā Taŧva* or Divine Light that escaped during the process of one *Paṛam Ātmā* getting made from another *Paṛam Ātmā* created *Paṛam* Light and began to spread in the *Vāyu Mandàḷ.*

"*Sañkalps* began to take place. The very wish to create from one to two to twelve to 108 and so on itself was a subtle desire and through that the *Paṛam Māhā Taŧva* or Divine Light was created and things spread. The desire to create began to take subtle force and thus, *Paṛam Ākāś,* the Supreme Space element came about. A very Supreme Space element but nonetheless the Divine Light began to break-up into elements.

"So, till the time the 16000 *Ātmās* started to be created, the *Paṛam Māhā Tatva* emerged. Then from 16000 souls came the nine-lakh souls and during this period the *Paṛam Ākāś Tatva* or Supreme Space element was created. So from the *Paṛam Māhā Tatva* or Divine Light, the *Paṛam Ākāś Tatva*, Supreme Space or Ether element was created. So till this stage the Divine Light was still around 95 per cent and Supreme Space element was five per cent. But even now the *Sañkalps* were happening in the most infinitely subtle form. Thus, till the first nine-lakh souls there existed *Paṛam Māhā Tatva* or Divine Light and *Paṛam Ākāś Tatva* or the Supreme Space or Ether Element. This is all in the *Bēj Rūp Avasthā* that is the State of Sprouting or the Burgeoning stage."

I so needed a cigarette. Where is the main nicotine *tatva* when one needs it? Fortunately liquefied nicotine in the form of tea was served.

"What is the meaning of *Avasthā*?"

"*Avasthā* means Stage."

"It means 'The Journey or the Stages of The Soul'," informed *Bapuji*. "Stage meaning the level of the soul or the celestial degree of the soul and we call or term it as *Kaḷā;* like 16 *Kaḷā*, 14 *Kaḷā*, etc. *Kaḷā* also refers to its *Gūṇa* or attributes and characteristics of the soul. Each stage or *Kaḷā* has a different composition of Divine Light and Supreme Elements and then as we move downward, the loss of the Supreme Element being filled up with just the normal three elements and then a further loss to just normal five elements, as we know it now. As the five elements grow the Supreme Elements reduce, till a time comes when there's barely one per cent of *Paṛam Māhā Tatva* and basically then it is just the normal five elements; thus, the spiritual loss and the loss of power.

"*Kaḷā* means stage or Celestial Degree or spiritual power. From the Supreme Power House, 5.5 per cent of *Paṛam, Paṛam, Paṛam Pṛakāś* or Divine Light was dissipated to create these nine-lakh souls. We call this stage 16 *Kaḷā* or the 16th Celestial Degree. So, first was the Absolute Authority, then *Paṛam Pitā* and now we have reached the first nine-lakh souls. This stage of nine-lakh souls is the 16th Celestial Degree or 16 *Kaḷā*. The Supreme Abode was shining and self-illuminating in the mercury-like white and pure light, but because of the golden colour of Supreme Space or Ether i.e. *Paṛam Ākāś Tatva*, souls began to descend to the causal world or *Mūḷ Vatan*, in which 'The Golden Age' dawns. Souls had to come down as the Supreme Abode could not accommodate more than nine-lakh souls.

"Thus the Golden Age is till the 15 *Kaḷā* which is the causal world also called the *Mūḷ Vatan*. The souls began to take on a causal body. And then when two-crore souls were created by the 14 *Kaḷā*, the first signs of the astral world was seen, which is called the *Sūkśṃ Vatan*. Due to the phenomenal increase of souls, and thus the beginning of desires, within each soul, the golden colour of the light body changed into the silver white subtle body and thus this is also called the Subtle World.

"So from 16 *Kaḷā* to 15 *Kaḷā* to 14 *Kaḷā*, in a similar manner from 9-lakh souls to 18-lakh souls, 18-lakh souls to 36-lakh souls, 36-lakhs to 72-lakh souls and then from 72-lakh souls to two-crore souls were created. *Mūl Vatan* or the causal world ended and *Sūkśṃ Vatan* or the astral world began. *Paṛam Vāyu* (Supreme Air) and *Paṛam Agni* (Supreme Fire) came about during the 14 *Kaḷā*. Why did *Paṛam Vāyu* or the Supreme Air Element and *Paṛam Agni*, the Supreme Fire Element come about? Because the speed at which the souls began to multiply through *Sañkalps*, which though were in a subtle form, nonetheless had increased, and one does need wind to fan the fire to spread all over?

"By the 14 *Kaḷā*, Supreme Light got reduced to around 70 per cent and *Paṛam Tatva* that is the Supreme Space, Wind and Fire elements increased to around 30 per cent. Thus one can see the drop of Supreme Divine Radiance and Divine Light or the *Paṛam, Paṛam, Paṛam Pṛakāś* and *Māhā Tatva* and the increase in other elements like Supreme Space, Wind and Fire. Thus one can see, on such a subtle stage itself, the loss of Supreme Power taking place. Where did the real Power go? It went in the creation of *Paṛam Tatvas* and the two-crore *Ātmās*. "So from here the astral bodies started to form and with the astral bodies forming, stronger *Sañkalps* or desires began to emerge as now the power of the Supreme Elements had increased to nearly thirty per cent of the soul composition and the Divine Light had reduced to seventy per cent. Remember earlier the souls were *Nirākāri* or formless in *Paṛam Dhām* or the Supreme Abode and in the *Nirākāri* state, the *Ātmā* was made of only Divine Light or *Māhā Tatva*. Here in the *Mūḷ Vatan* and *Sūkśṃ Vatan*, the causal and astral worlds, the *Paṛam Tatvas* were created. From Supreme Space came Supreme Wind or Air that enveloped the soul on all four sides. As we started to arrive in the subtle world, the *Paṛam Agni Tatva* came about and then everything began to multiply and the number of souls increased to two-crore. Remember when desires began to multiply due to Prime elements, automatically desires created a fire within and that is when *Paṛam Agni Tatva* came about. When there is fire inside the *Ātmās*, even if it is in the most subtle form, like 00.001 per cent, more desires start to multiply and with greater desires negativity takes birth.

"*Bhāvnas* that is emotions began from this point. The initial *Bhāvna* was 'he looks like me, so he is like me, so he is my brother', so the soul for the first time became soul-conscious of its individuality. The soul-conscious subtle bodies began to grow. Remember *Paṛam Agni Taṫva* doesn't mean that there is fire like our normal fire element. But it is a state of having wishes and desires, that's when emotions or *Bhāvnas* come in. But bear in mind that in this stage there is still no negativity. But because this stage is so subtle, so refined and so pure even chaste *Bhāvna* or emotion itself is negative compared to being in a state of unadulterated bliss and no desires.

"So from 14th Celestial Degree we came down to 13th Celestial Degree or 13 *Kaḷā*. That's when more *Sañkalps* started to come about and the speed of desires also increased. As the speed increased, the number of *Sañkalps* further increased and this is when creation started to take place and increase in number. How did creation come about? Certain souls began to be more with each other than the rest of the other souls. They began to feel a certain sense of oneness with their group than with the others. Imagine you have two-crore and more souls and thus more and more groups began to form. When groups began to form the need to stay together arose. And what did they create? They created the first houses or colonies for each one to stay in the astral world. So in the 13 *Kaḷā*, the Divine Light got further reduced and there was a loss of power of the Divine Light and the soul now contained 64 per cent to 61 per cent of Divine Light when compared to the earlier 70 per cent and the *Paṛam Taṫvas* gained power and increased to nearly 40 per cent. Thus, the Absolute Authority's Supreme Divine Radiance and Divine Light began to further reduce and the power of the Prime Elements began to increase.

"This way *Kaḷā* to *Kaḷā*, or Celestial fall to Celestial fall, by the time creation came to the 9th Celestial Degree or 9 *Kaḷā*, the two-crore souls had increased to 2.74-crore souls. Soul population did not increase as much as the subtle desires increased but in a pure manner. Remember we are still talking about *Paṛam Tatvas* or Supreme Elements. So as souls got caught up in their desires and creations, the stage of 'the splitting-up of souls', for a while slowed down."

I took a break. Walked up to the road and sat down and watched the cars passing by. In all honesty all my life I have never cared much about the technicalities of spirituality. My spirituality began and ended with *Bābā Sai of Shirdi*. He was all the Celestial Degrees or *Kaḷās* for me. You must understand I am not the type to analyze spirituality. Also what you are reading is a far simpler version of the conversation I had with *Bapuji*. In short my mind was *Paṛam Fried* or supremely scrambled. When I returned I was handed a mug of steaming hot soup. We spoke about this and that and then got back to the darn *Kaḷās*.

"So till the 9 *Kaḷā* they spent their time in creating other worlds and thus they started to waste their power and they started to fall from Grace. Since they wasted power, they came into what we call is the Falling *Kaḷā*."

"Why is it called the Falling *Kaḷā*?" I inquired.

"That iṣ because from the 8 *Kaḷā*, for the first time, the soul which was male energy created through *Sañkalps*, the woman energy."

"Ahhhhh…The *Kaḷā* of trouble." I mused. Not good. Not good.

I remembered this very popular joke we used to laugh a lot about when we were kids. It went something like this; First God made the Heavens and then He rested. Then God made the Earth and then He rested. Then God made men and then He rested. And then God made women and since then neither God nor men have ever rested.

I know. I know. I can be profound at times.

13

We took a short break and resumed. Though the philosophy is completely *Bapuji's*, *Anant* and *Sakshi* began to converse more now.

"Till now we have tried to understand how we separated from the Absolute Authority, the infinite world, travelling from the *Bayhud* or infinite *ŚivaŚakti*, to different abodes, different levels and different elemental worlds. One thing that is clear is that all this was not destined but it was happening gradually with time and with no one's particular will. But another thing that is of importance is that, creation works at its own pace, and things evolve or change slowly. We have spent infinite ages, several thousands of light years, beyond one's imagination and it took infinite time for souls to descend from different levels.

"Also each Celestial Degree is like a different world, having variety of life and colours, inexpressible for the simple reason, there are certain things that can only be experienced and cannot be described."

I guess this is very true. *Avatār Meher Bābā* has often, along with other Masters and Prophets, made it clear that the spiritual world cannot really be described. It has to be experienced. The path to experience is through the Grace of the Master, by going within, becoming one with the Breath and through meditation. It is then that the astral and causal bodies travel through the various dimensions of the spirit world, soak in the environment and experience its varied dimensions first hand. Even then, coming back into the body, it becomes virtually impossible to describe in words the magnificence and ethereal beauty so recently experienced. It is like trying to describe the beauty of the rainbow and various different colours, to somebody who has been born visually impaired; truly difficult if not impossible. The way to go about this would be through meditation, going beyond the physical visual limitation, and in the spirit body, soar and experience the rainbow and the sunrise and sunset and if a man, then might as-well admire the beauty of the dangerous specie too, and then come back into the body; once again unable to describe it but with the knowledge of it... Back to *Sakshi*.

"We keep on changing the composition of our existence, first was *Paṛam Pṛakāś* or Supreme Divine Radiance to *Māhā Tatva* or the Divine Light as an element to *Paṛam Tatvas* and then eventually to the general *Tatvas,* in the astral plane and then the five *Tatvas* or elements on the physical plane. As we descend we start coming into the negative element from Supreme Divine Radiance to *Paṛam Tatvas*."

Please understand *Paṛam Tatvas* aren't negative but when compared to the Supreme Divine Radiance and Divine Light, *Paṛam Tatvas* is a step down the graph, and thus if Supreme Divine Radiance and Divine Light is positive, then Prime Elements become negative in nature.

"Now from 9 *Kaḷā* or the 9th Celestial Degree to *Zero Kaḷā*. Of course that is a long way off as the approximate distance from the 9th Celestial Degree, from our earth, is about 1,53,600 *Arab* or trillion light years. Now in the 9 *Kaḷā,* Divine Light is just between 29 per cent to 49 per cent and the soul composition for the first time has more *Paṛam Tatvas* than *Paṛam Light*, standing at 51 per cent to 71 per cent. As we keep thinking and creating and using our *Sañkalps* and manifesting our desires, the fall from Grace is quicker. The more we think and desire, the greater the amount of *Śakti* the soul begins to loose or consume and waste away. The souls began to lose energy and the Divine Light began to dwindle away and the ratio of *Paṛam Tatvas* began to increase. In the 8 *Kaḷā* we were continuously in the process of thoughts and creating different worlds, life, galaxies, souls and other numerous things as per the need, requirement, emotions and feelings."

Hello, it's me again. The reason why the 8 *Kaḷā* is so important is that *Paṛam Puruś* was made of Divine Light and the three Prime Elements of Ether or Space, Air or Wind and Fire. From the *Paṛam Māhā Tatva* the soul composition became more *Paṛam Tatvas* and then slowly began to become normal or general *Tatvas* though still in the spirit plane. But the most important aspect of the 8 *Kaḷā*, apart from woman energy being created, was that by the end of 8 *Kaḷā*, *Paṛam* Light disappeared and *Paṛam Tatvas* became 80 to 99 per cent and for the first time General or Gross *Tatvas* came about with a minimum of one per cent and maximum of 20 per cent in the soul composition. General or gross *Tatvas*,(Space corrected)that include the three normal elements of Either, Air and Fire entered in the 8 *Kaḷā*.

"Now the 8th Celestial Degree was almost 38,400 *Arab* light years from the earth, with 80 to 99 per cent of *Paṛam Tatvas* and one to 20 per cent of Gross or General *Tatvas* or elements. The per cent of the gross *Tatva* means composition of three elements, Either, Air and Fire. In this also, as we gradually fall due to increasing *Sañkalps*, the per cent of the *Ākāś* element decreases as compared to the other two elements, which gradually increase in percentage thus bringing about heaviness, and leaving us getting more and more occupied in thoughts and creation. But still, this stage, with different elements, has immense beauty with a variety of colours, flowers, life…actually it is like paradise that we talk about. Everything looks beautiful, attractive, peaceful, but souls are still falling unknowingly due to the increase of thoughts, wants, desires and more creation. Each world is different from the other, life is different and if we have to reach or go there, we have to transform our elements. To be able to sustain in that world we have to adapt to the elements that exist in that world." Informed *Sakshi*.

"*Betā*," *Bapuji* began to speak. "What they are really trying to say is that due to more and more *Sañkalps*, the *Paṛam Tatvas* that were there, slowly…very slowly but very surely began to convert into normal *Tatvas*. How did that happen? As more souls began to be created *Paṛam Ākāś*, *Vāyu*, and *Agni Tatvas* began to increase but in the end of 9 *Kaḷā* and the beginning of 8 *Kaḷā* the balance shifted more towards *Paṛam Tatvas* and less towards Divine Light. So these souls still were *Paṛam Puruś* or Prime Souls but till the end of 9 *Kaḷā* and beginning of 8 *Kaḷā*, there were no women… *Ruzbeh* you laughing like this is making me laugh too! Thankfully *Mataji* is not here." *Bapuji* spoke with a twinkle in his eyes. "So, earlier the souls were still *Paṛam Puruś* or Prime Souls only, and they were soul conscious but when they decided to create the woman energy, from soul conscious, they, for the first time became body conscious. That is why the ending of the 9 *Kaḷā* and the beginning of the 8 *Kaḷā* is very important because it is here that in the *Paṛam Puruś* or Supreme Male, an extremely subtle *Sañkalp* began to grow and that was to create or give birth to *Prakruti* or the woman energy and nature. Just as *Lord Śiva* created *Mā Śakti*, like that *Paṛam Puruś* created *Prakruti*.

"Why did he create the woman energy now and not before… because the *Paṛam Pṛakāś* and the *Māhā Tatva* began to reduce and for the first time the ratio of *Paṛam Tatvas* increased. So now predominately, even though very marginally, the *Paṛam Tatvas* had a greater hold over the souls than the *Māhā Tatva* or Divine Light. Because what exists in the *Vāyu Mandāḷ* or environment is also what exists in the body. Divine Light was reduced to 49 per cent and *Paṛam Taṫvas* increased to 51 per cent, so by two per cent *Paṛam Taṫvas* became heavier in the soul composition. And thus from the end of 9 *Kaḷā* and beginning of the 8 *Kaḷā*, the astral body of three elements, as we know it evolved.

"So *betā*, now the *Ātmā* has made a *Sañkalp* that from *Puruś* or male 'I want to create *Prakruti* or the female'. So virtually in the end of 9 *Kaḷā* and beginning of the 8 *Kaḷā* women were created."

"Is that why you have called this stage the *Falling Kaḷā*?" I inquired with a straight face.

"You are going to create problems for me *Ruzbeh*. Women organizations will be up in arms and I will send them to you." Saying this he chuckled. "Anyway so up till now everybody was soul-conscious in a state of *Paṛam Ānand, Nijānand Swarūpam* which means Pure Supreme Bliss, Image of the One in Self Delight or the Divine Joyful Image of the Own Self…"

"Basically earlier all were relaxed and staying in peace."

"Yes as they were soul-conscious, but once from soul-conscious the *Ātmā* became body conscious, the Fall from Grace really accelerated, because 'I and You' started. So the population that was around 2.74 crore in the 9-*Kaḷā* became approximately five and a half-crore virtually in the beginning of the 8 *Kaḷā*. So now that the Male and Female energy came about a sort of competition began. Till now what was all Oneness began to wither away into 'me and my' creations and 'you and your' creations. But remember even now at this stage it was very subtle; very pure but yet not as pure as before but still pure. Now *Sañkalps* were taken to make the woman creation happy; especially as she has been created out of his *Sañkalps* and he brought her into the world. A world that we know of in the physical form but still in the astral dimension started to take shape in its extreme subtle form."

Remember even the Bible says that Eve was created out of Adam; from the poor chap's rib, if I am not wrong.

"So, at the end of stage 9 and beginning of the 8 *Kaḷā*, the minutest of the minutest subtle *Swarūp* of the five-elemental world began. The *Atī Sūkśṃ* world or the extremely subtle astral world came into existence."

"So *Bapuji*, this world that we know of, the first images of it in the spirit world began here? The astral world similar to that of the physical world as we know it, started here at the end of 9th Celestial Degree and beginning of 8th Celestial Degree?"

"Yes *betā* but it was very beautiful and very subtle. So what did everyone do out here, they all started to make their own worlds. What did they make, they started to create their own *Brähṁāñḍs* or worlds or galaxies. So, to impress the other half, subtle competition commenced. You have made a beautiful world, I will make two hundred such beautiful worlds and the other person will say I will make five hundred such beautiful worlds and the next one will go ahead and make five thousand. This continued and more and more of the *Paṛam Pṛakāś* and *Māhā Tatva* began to be dissipated and more and more *Paṛam Tatvas* began to increase in the *Vāyu Mandàḷ* and thus in each soul. Imagine our *Milky Way* is their one *Brähṁāñḍ* of those times, so then trillions of *Brähṁāñḍs* were created... like we produce children and they keep growing... and then our power and wealth we keep distributing and dividing amongst our children, similarly, power began to be distributed and began to dissipate.

"So there was a minimum 80 to 99 per cent *Paṛam Tatvas* then. The population increased by the end of 8 *Kaḷā* to nearly 6.5 crore but there were countless *Brähṁāñḍs* or worlds, truly beautiful worlds created, but the loss of power came from competition and the insatiable creation of outwardly objects. So at the end of 8 *Kaḷā, Paṛam* Light disappeared, *Parma Taŧvas* took a massive leap and became 80 to 99 per cent and for the first time General *Taŧvas* came about with a minimum of one per cent and maximum of 20 per cent. General *Taŧvas* means elements without Divine Light; which means by the end of this time, in the 8 *Kaḷā, Paṛam Light* did not exist."

So basically, women entered and *Paṛam Light* was shown the door. Classic!

For all the stuff I talk about women, the fact is that they are the stronger and the more spiritual specie. Yes, they operate only from the heart chakra and thus often make the men want to uproot trees, apart from their own hair, is another matter, but nature had faith in the female of the specie to entrust them to continue the lineage of all creation, which speaks a lot for the selflessness that most of them inherently possess. Most women have a certain sense of character and ethical values that is on a higher level than the male of the specie. Of course, there are exceptions to all rules. Exceptions like, some men do grow up and some women don't want to possess your soul.

"Tell me more about this business of 'womanhood' or *Prakruti* coming forth from *Puruś*?" I asked *Bapuji.*

"What is the meaning of *Prakruti*? What is the definition of *Prakruti*? *Prakruti* means nature. Nature means *Svabhāv* or character and *Sanskār* means value system and conditioning. So, how was your nature initially? The way in which your nature was earlier is exactly how your nature will be in the present. It is only with *Sañkalps* that *Srushti* or the world is created and the *Vāyu Mandàḷ* that is the world of environment and vibration is made. If you have positive thinking then all around you, you will find a positive atmosphere. And if you are positive then the one who comes in front of you too imbibes a bit of your positivity. You can create an aura that spans over hundred feet. It can travel from twenty-feet to even two-hundred feet or even around the whole world if you so wish. So the more positive you are, the people around you will be more and so the atmosphere will be full of positivity. *Paṛam Pṛakāś* or Supreme Divine Radiance is one who we call the Almighty Authority.

"How were the souls earlier? They were *Nirākāri*. They transformed into the *Ākāri* or one with form and they started to get a shape. After acquiring a form, they obtained a subtle body of *Paṛam Tatvas* in the subtle world and from the *Puruś* the *Prakruti* was created."

"Why did *Prakruti* emerge out of *Puruś*? Shouldn't it have been the other way round?"

"It is so, because till that time, the soul's body-combination was 51 per cent *Paṛam* Light and 49 per cent *Paṛam Tatvas*. Now that means in each *Ātmā*, the power of the Absolute Authority, was still more than the elements within the soul. But during the 8 *Kaḷā*, the Absolute Authority's power reduced, when compared to elements, in each soul. The body combination changed to 49 per cent *Paṛam* Light and 51 per cent *Paṛam Tatva*. The level of *Paṛàm Tatvas* increased, thus from the body, the other body emerged. That other body that emerged is called *Prakruti*. It is His nature. From His nature His body came out. So, that is *Puruś* and *Prakruti*."

Which means technically the woman entity hasn't really come out from the male being. First there was the *Ātmā*, which basically is a composition of varying Supreme Divine Radiance and Divine Light as well as Prime Elements. Supreme Divine Radiance and Divine Light denote the Absolute Authority's presence in each soul. When His presence in each soul became less than the *Paṛam Tatvas*, there seemed to be a kind of burst and the soul parted and two bodies emerged, one male and one female. So initially the soul was sexless and when the composition of *Paṛam Taṫvas* increased more than that of the Supreme Divine Radiance and Divine Light, the soul split-up into male and female energy.

Maybe the *Big Bang* theory in reality took place when the soul parted and two distinct sexes got created. Back to *Bapuji*.

"So, between the female and the male bodies there was a kind of getting along but still there really was no distinction. And then countless worlds came about and in the astral as-well-as gross material or physical world *Anant Koti Brāhṁāñḍs, Māhā Brāhṁāñḍs, Paṛam Māhā Brāhṁāñḍs*, Suns and *Māhā* Suns, *Māhā Māhā Sūryas*, all of these began to be created due to subtle competition."

I can imagine the woman energy telling the exhausted male energy: *Bhala uska galaxy meray galaxy say bada kaise*? Never! Swāmi, make my galaxy bigger please.

"So with competition more and more creation came about. All this was made of *Paṛam Taṫvas* and later on with a combination of *Paṛam Taṫvas* and *gross Taṫvas*. In the stage of *Paṛam Taṫvas* or Prime Elements as soon as one makes a *Sañkalp* or a wish, things materialize. Since we all are soul conscious, each and every thought occurring inside each *Ātmā* or soul would manifest and come true. I'll give you an example: there are many people in the world, but does the face of any two people match? Why is there a difference? It is because inside every soul, the *Svabhāv* and *Sañskārs* that's nature and conditioning or soul journey are different. Their astral bodies are different. And because the astral forms are different which are based on their subtle forms, which in turn are based on *Prakruti* – thus their subtle form is different. On the basis of their *Prakruti* each one's gross body is made. Can you imagine how many multiple combinations would have occurred till now? In fact there were innumerable combinations of the

Paṛam Tatvas too. Each *Brāhmāñḍ* is made of *Paṛam Tatvas* and in each *Brāhmāñḍ* you can see a variety of colours and combinations among *Paṛam Tatvas.* Thus they continued to create multiple *Brāhmāñḍs* below the 9 *Kaḷā* especially in the 8 and 7 *Kaḷā.* Now, when power is being used to its maximum, and if one does not like the *Brāhmāñḍ* then they would make a *Sañkalp* and the whole *Brāhmāñḍ* would go through a major transformation, which means that the complete *Brāhmāñḍ* would be absolutely dissolved and a new one would be created. Time and again, the *Paṛam Tatvas'* energy was used and this would result in the *Paṛam Tatva* disappearing or being depleted and *gross Tatvas* increasing. Just like when we have more children the number of divisions and shares of one's property increase. Similarly, the power waste here became so much that gradually trillions and hundreds of hundred billion galaxies and worlds came about and that is how eventually we all descended to the world of Zero *Kaḷā.* It must have been infinite time that passed because it is not easy to measure."

So it was decided that we would talk about the other *Kaḷās* the next day. The topic went on to the creation of our planet, Mother Earth.

"*Śiva Nirākār* means a *Bindi,* a dot. Formless *Śiva* is a speck, a dot. Him we call *Śivātmā. Śiva* from *Nirākār* or formless, became one with a form or *Ākāri.* And *Śiva* created *Śakti* and came to *Śivpuri*; *Ardh Nāreśwar,* means half *Śiva*-half *Śakti.*

"From *Ardh Nāreśwar, ŚivaŚakti* created *Viśnu.* And *Viśnu* created *Mā Laxmi,* so they came to *Viśnupuri.* From the navel of *Viśnu* emerged *Brāhmā.* Then *Brāhmā* through *Sañkalps* created *Sṛuśti* or this world as we know.

"*Brāhmā* initially created the *Sapta Ruśis* or seven sages; we see Them in the night sky symbolically, don't we? Symbolically, represented in the sky as 'The Archer' where the last star directly points to the North Pole Star anytime of the year, where the seven stars keep on circling the North Star.

"The seven *Ruśis* made the seven *Loks* or dimensions. Even the *Muslims* say: 'Where does *Allah Talla* stay? *Khudā Tālā Toh Sātvey Āsmān Se Bhi Pareh Rehtā Hai*'. Where does *Allah* stay? Much beyond the Seventh Sky or the Seventh Dimension. '*Sātvey Āsmān Sey Pareh*' that is 'Above the Seventh Sky or Dimension', which means *Nirākāri*. When they talk about *Nirākār* they talk with reference to our *Brāhmāṅḍ*. No one can ever talk about the *Nirākāri* or the Formless World – the Infinite World.

"Firstly the seven *Loks* or worlds were created. Then the *Manu Sṛuśti* or Man World was made. Who created the *Manu Sṛuśti*? Adam and Hawa or Adam and Eve they are called by many names. We shall call them *Manu* and *Satarupa. Manu* and *Satarupa* on this *Bhu Lok,* made the *Dhàṛti* and created the *Manu Sṛuśti* or the human race.

"Now time moves with great speed and on earth we have the *Sat Yug, Treytā Yug, Dvāpar Yug* and the *Kal Yug*. On earth when *Sat Yug* is in progression, all is positive; during *Treytā Yug Ram Avatār* took place, at the end of *Dvāpar Yug Kṛiṣna Avatār* and many other *Avatārs* came to remove evil and let truth triumph.

"Whenever there is *Adharmā* or injustice on earth, Lord *Viśnu,* will come down to remove injustice and evil. Thus, came about the twenty-four *Avatārs* of Lord *Viśnu.* Lord *Viśnu* is not here on earth, but He sends but He sends one of His cells down, who becomes an *Avatār* here and Lord *Viśnu* keeps on getting His work done through Him, sitting right up there.

"So, on the earth four *Yugs* take place. Let's take the basic concept into consideration. How much time does *Kal Yug* take? *Kal Yug* lasts for four-lakh and thirty two thousand years. Double of that time is taken by *Dvāpar*

Yug. Three times more than that is *Treytā* and four times more is *Satyug*. So, the total time taken collectively by all four *Yugs* is forty three-lakh and twenty-thousand years (43,20,000 years). During the time-period of *Kalyug,* many fights, quarrels and wars take place and the complete *Vāyu Mandàḷ* gets polluted.

"Note that inside every speck of the *Vāyu Mandàḷ,* the *Vāyu* element has cells and small ions. Inside each and every speck or *Aṇu* of the *Vāyu Mandàḷ* whatever is being said and spoken, felt and thought gets recorded. That is inside each speck, each cell of the *Vāyu Mandàḷ*. For instance all that *Kṛiṣna* used to sing or the music He would play on the flute, five thousand years ago, can be reproduced. All that recording is available in the Air, it's all thrown in the element of *Vāyu* – it's all present. In each and every *Kaṇ* and *Aṇu,* that is – a speck and an atom of the element of air, all that is ever done, spoken and witnessed – All is ever present.

"Why did the *Vāyu Mandàḷ* get polluted and corrupted? Each one's *Sañkalps* started to get negative. As the various *Satyug, Dvāpar, Treytā* and *Kal Yugs,* arrived the *Vāyu Mandàḷ* started to get negative. In that there is no fault of anyone. The *Vāyu Mandàḷ* tends to get polluted. First it becomes one per cent negative, then five per cent, ten per cent negative and then it becomes ninety-nine per cent negative.

"So today, if you want to change or transform the world, you have to transform the *Vāyu Mandàḷ*. Fill the current *Vāyu Mandàḷ* with *Paṛam Tatvas* and give it positive vibrations. Give the affirmation that 'let there be *Paṛam, Paṛam, Paṛam Sukh Śanti*...Happiness and Peace for all in all creations'.

"In fact, we are just about to start the process of transforming the complete air and atmosphere, the *Vāyu Mandàḷ*. The *Sañkalp* that says: *"Bayhud ke Viśwa Mein,*

Bayhuđ ki Paṛam, Paṛam, Paṛam Sukh Śanti Ho". In the World of the Infinite, Let the Purest of Pure Joy and Peace prevail. Only then the *Paṛam Taŧvas* from up will come down. The *Paṛam Taŧva* is up there for sure. As the *Sūkśṃ Jagat,* that is the astral or subtle world started to develop mainly in the 8 *Kaḷā*, the *Paṛam Taŧvas* started to come down. So the *Paṛam Taŧvas* are lying up there and if brought down now, then the current *Taŧvas* could initiate positive thinking and the whole world would be bathed in positive healing.

"Now on earth, the four *Yugas* got over and done with, so that's called Half *Prälai*. The meaning of *Prälai* is *Vinaś* or destruction. Only the *Satya Pradhān Ātmās* remain after any sort of *Prälai*. *Satya Pradhān* means positive. The negative ones are destroyed. Just like that, seventy one times, *Ardh Prälai* or half *Prälai* takes place. We call one cycle of four *Yugas,* one *Yugāntar*. Like that 71 *Yugāntars* take place that is when the Total *Prälai* or the complete destruction on earth takes place, that's when *Manu Satàṛupa's* time gets over. So, when total *Vinaś* or destruction takes place, not a single human soul will remain."

I so, so, so wanted a smoke.

14

Meher and I were in some mall. According to me malls are the physical manifestation of hell, the worst *Lok* of them all. Though I spend a lot of time in malls, thanks to my shopaholic five-year old, I wouldn't miss a night of sleep, if I never had to step into a mall ever. Of course like any father is well aware, malls like politicians are here to stay. So *Meher* took time deciding what to buy or what not to buy. She wanted a Barbie doll sitting on a unicorn, with purple hair. Oh Boy it was going to be a long haul.

Anyway after a while, a long while, where I was made to personally examine countless different types of Barbie dolls, and boy the chap who manufactures them has a vivid imagination and clothing sense bordering on the ludicrous, we settled for *Barbie The Swan Song*, a DVD, which mercifully had on its cover a very healthy looking unicorn with a purple tail. Then it was time to eat something. Long story short, a glass of water fell, spilling water all over the table. After we settled on another table, *Meher* looked at me.

"Why is water liquid?"

"Eh? What?"

"Why does water wet everything? Why is it liquid?"

"God made it that way love." I am big on getting God involved in all scientific inquires. I don't know Jack where science or most things are concerned but I also am certain our Lord is a whiz kid on all this scientific and electronic stuff.

"Why couldn't He have made water hard?"

"Water is meant to quench our thirst. And the main essence of water is... to be wet... I guess. Like the main essence of fire is heat. And the main essence of daughters is to make their fathers climb-up walls on and off." This is what happens when fathers copy all the way through school and college and are reading comic books and novels when the clueless science teacher is yapping on-and-on about creation and the essence of things.

"Ok. And why do bats only come out at night."

"I don't know love. Maybe they sleep very late in the day."

"How can they see at night dad? The way they fly here and there, never in a straight way, I don't think they can see very well."

"Uh... .. I don't think bats can see love. They can feel the vibrations of things and thus can navigate or move about. That's how God made them love."

"God is too funny. Why didn't He just give bats eyes to see Daddy, instead of making them feel things? That way these bats wouldn't scare all of us."

"I will inform God about your observation about Bats and water when I meet Him next. Now eat your darn chocolate and let's scoot from here."

So next day I was back with *Bapuji.* Why would the cosmos want me to write a book on evolution when I couldn't even give rational answers to my five-year old?

"So now when we enter the 7 *Kaḷā* or 7th Celestial Degree, the world was made of *Paṛam Taŧva*, the body was made of *Paṛam Taŧva* and *general or Gross Taŧva* and the *Vāyu Mañdal* too essentially was made of *Paṛam Taŧva*. Creation abounded and worlds were created. It was just like how one imagines heaven; beautiful and like the land of fairytales. The most beautiful creations were brought about. With just one thought one could create and another thought one could erase one's own creation, and immediately recreate with one more thought. There was immense *Paṛam Sukh* or Supreme Joy in this stage. Above the 9 *Kaḷā*, there was *Paṛam Śañti* or Supreme Peace. The moment *Pṛakṛuti* in the form of nature and womanhood began, Supreme Peace got converted to Supreme Joy slowly and by the 7 *Kaḷā* only *Paṛam Sukh* or Joy prevailed. Thus, very subtle negativity began to manifest. And then as one slowly descended to various lower *Kaḷās*, *Paṛam Sukh* got diluted to only *Sukh* and then the negative element of *Sukh* which is sadness or misery entered in the form of *Dukh*." Informed *Bapuji*.

Tolerate my blabber for a while. According to me, basically this is the age-old truth or reality of positive and negative. As Prophet *Zarathustra* introduced the concept of heaven and hell, He said that wherever there is Light, there will be darkness or the shadow. So if we start with positive and negative, *Paṛam Dhām* was the positive and the 16 *Kaḷā* though so supremely divine, became its negative. If you notice there was nothing negative in 16 *Kaḷā* — in fact 16 *Kaḷā* is called *Saṁpūṛṇa* or complete within itself — but compared to the Supreme Abode which was only *Paṛam Pṛakāś* or Supreme Divine Radiance, 16 *Kaḷā* was negative; which means that while creating *Paṛam Pitā*, the Founding Father of the Infinite, there was a slight loss of *Paṛam Pṛakāś* and for the first time *Paṛam Māhā Taťva* or the Prime Divine Light as an element got created. So compared to Infinite Divine Radiance, even the *Paṛam Māhā Taťva* that one would call Divine Light is negative. Can you imagine the law of creation? When there is something positive, there has to be something negative, howsoever subtle. So then from *Paṛam Māhā Taťva* came *Paṛam Ākāś* which is the subtlest of the Pure Space Element but compared to the Divine Light, it still is negative. From *Paṛam Māhā Taťva* and *Paṛam Ākāś* emerged *Paṛam Vāyu* and then through that surfaced *Paṛam Agni,* together called *Paṛam Tatvas.* Even here the *Paṛam Māhā Tatva* was much more in proportion till we came to the end of 9 and the beginning of 8 *Kaḷā* where the proportion of *Paṛam Tatvas* increased. And then with the *Paṛam Tatvas* came about Gross or General *Tatva* but still in the astral world it was very sublime, though negative compared to the *Paṛam Tatvas.* It was then that the *General Tatvas* became the five normal physical five general *Tatvas* or elements which is still positive if you consider the elements in hell, down under, in the various *Loks* and then there is positive and negative even in hell as, till you come to the *Pātāl Lok,* which though is not a very rocking place where positivity is considered but even here it is more positive than the crores of beyond the beyond hells existing beyond the *Pātāl Lok.* So there is positive and negative in everything?

There is also hierarchy; there always was, always is and always will be hierarchy. Call it positive and negative. Higher and lower, up and down. Thought and word. Word and action. In our individual graph the glowing Causal body is the Rock star. So if the causal body is positive then in comparison the astral body becomes negative, which is positive when compared to the physical body, which is positive when compared to the body that has no life but even a corpse is more positive than a rotting cadaver, which can still be considered positive as it still feeds some sort of life when compared to ashes when the body is burnt away, which is nothing but dust and mingles with dust. So our causal body is at the top and dust is at the bottom of the graph (am sure it can go down further) of this hierarchy of an individual. But when compared to where one originated from, even the causal body becomes negative as there is a hierarchy even above one's individuality. Did you come from the 2-crore, and where did they come from, the 9-lakhs, and where did those chaps come from till you come to the 108, and even there the 108th soul may have come out from the 9th soul and the 9th soul came out from the 2nd and the 2nd came out from the 1st who came from the Founding Father of the Infinite who came from the Absolute Authority. In each stage there's a positive compared to the one subtle rung below and thus inevitably making it negative when compared to the one above. So this positive and negative was, is and will always be there. And it exists within us too. This perpetual war between our very own dormant Godhood that exists within us and the active dark forces; even in right and wrong, good and bad, there are stages and demarcations. Something is always more or less positive or slightly more or less negative than something else. Why us? Take the Absolute Authority, whose power is All Encompassing and Eternal and Permanent. Compared to the Absolute Authority, even the Founding Father of the Infinite, has less power even though He is the Creator of all creation as we know it but when compared to the Absolute Authority even our Founding Father of the Infinite could slightly be wanting where the proportion of Supreme Divine Radiance is concerned. As I said, I kind-of like to ramble along.

"So from the end of the 9 and through the 8 and into the 7 *Kaḷā, Paṛam Sukh* or Prime Happiness existed. And in the earlier *Kaḷās* there existed *Paṛam Ānañd* which is Pure Joy. Happiness didn't exist so the shadow of sadness didn't exist too. Just Divine Joy or Ecstasy, and the higher you went upwards, you didn't feel even Prime Joy as there in the earliest *Kaḷās* you were *Paṛam Ānañd Swaṛūpam* or the Prime Form of Bliss and Liberating Peace. But from the 9 *Kaḷā* and through the 8 *Kaḷā, Paṛam Sukh* entered and you know there is a great deal of difference in *Ānañd* that is Bliss and *Sukh* that is Happiness." Spoke *Bapuji.*

I guess one can say that happiness is connected most

often with outwardly experiences. You are happy that your son is doing well in his career and at the age of forty-two you don't have to give him pocket money. Your daughter is married and blowing her husband's money (and not yours), as though it was going out of fashion or circulation. Your wife is in good health and all of a sudden has divined the power of silence. Your work is going on well. All this brings you happiness. It can't bring you bliss. Bliss and joy are deeper emotions. Joy is the smile in the eyes of a dog or a child when playing joyously or an infant's gurgle. Being in joy is to know that God is in Heaven and all is well with the world. It springs from the heart and spreads into the core of every cell and mingles into one's breath. There may be no real reason for this joy. It comes forth from some eternal source within and spreads into your very aura. It is the breath of the Master – the caress of the sublime.

"So how did this happiness come about? Imagine that you have through *Sañkalps* brought forth 100-crore creations. These 100-crore *Rachanas* or creations in the 7 *Kaḷā* are experiencing happiness. So if they are experiencing *Sukh*, then you as the Creator will experience collective happiness which is *Paṛam Sukh.* And how did they experience happiness, through the subtle *Indṛiyās* or the five astral sense organs. So when you have happiness automatically you need the five sense organs to experience it which included vision, hearing, smell, taste and touch. But this stage also has *Divya Dṛuśti,* meaning Divine Vision. You could eat, talk, walk, touch, but still were in the Divine Vision, thus though this is a considerable Fall from Grace, when you compare them with the 16 *Kaḷā*, you still are in a very subtle form." Informed *Bapuji.*

Sakshi began to speak.

"So gradually in the process of falling we reach the 7th Celestial Degree, which is approximately 19,200-trillion light years away from the 8th Celestial Degree, and over here, 65 to 80 per cent of the individual's composition was *Paṛam Tatva* and the *Gross Tatva* increased to 20 to 35 per cent. Slowly the Fire element began to increase, raising the bar of negativity in the *Ātmā* and also in their creation around. Fire means heat, heat means desires. The more we fall, the heavier our elements become. This continued in the 6 *Kaḷā*, which is about 9,600 trillion light years away from the 7 *Kaḷā*, where the soul composition was 50 to 65 per cent of *Paṛam Tatva* and 35 to 50 per cent of gross element.

"Three-elemental bodies began to be formed with extremely heavy elements within. Earlier the elements were light due to *Paṛam Pṛakāś* or Supreme Divine Radiance, the *Māhā Tatva* or the Divine Light and *Paṛam Tatva* which are the Prime Elements of Space, Air and Fire. Now the body began to get heavier, giving the souls, a feeling of being body conscious rather than soul conscious. This is because the Supreme Divine Radiance was completely missing from the 7 and 6 *Kaḷā* as-well-as the energy the soul derived from, *Paṛam Tatva* or Supreme Elements were reducing at an alarming pace, raising the proportion of gross and solid elements. The souls began to forget their original being and now nothing was in control.

"By the time they descended to the 5th Celestial Degree or *Kaḷā*, which was approximately 4,800 light years away, the soul-body composition became, just 35 to 50 per cent of *Paṛam Tatva* and 50 to 65 per cent of *Gross Tatva*. The 4th Celestial Degree, 2,400 trillion light years from the 5th Celestial Degree is so important because the *Gross Tatva Tatva* at 65 to 75 per cent increased way above even the *Paṛam Tatva* which stood at an alarming low of just 25 to 35 per cent. In this 4 *Kaḷā* the final straw from the Fall of Grace took place. The souls began to descent at a furious pace, as they began to lose control over thoughts and desires; as the *Paṛam Ākāś Tatva* began to reduce in proportion to the other

Tatvas, Param as well as Gross. When *Ākāś Tatva* reduces, then the individual loses the ability to think clearly and be calm, and the elemental forces and the environment push the soul further down. The sad part of this is that though the soul is descending further down to *Zero Kaḷā,* it is oblivious of its fall, as even now everything looks beautiful and the ability to create, though slower, is still present in the *Sūkśṃ Ātmās* or the astral bodies.

"It would take 1,200 trillion light years to reach the 3rd Celestial Degree, which further witnessed an increase in the gross elements, which reached a level of 75 to 85 per cent and the *Paṛam Tatva* reduced to 15 to 25 per cent. Here, the Space Element or the element of Ether, in the soul-body structure further got reduced but everybody seemed to be blissfully unaware of their fall.

"The 2nd Celestial Degree brought about a composition of 85 to 90 percent of *Gross Tatva* and just 10 to 15 per cent of *Paṛam Tatva*, and it was about 300 trillion light years away from the 3rd *Kaḷā*. The 1st Celestial Degree had *Gross Tatva* of almost 90 to 94 per cent and the *Paṛam Tatva* reduced to just 6 to 10 per cent. In this *Kaḷā* the complete shape and role model of what was to appear on earth came about. But you must understand that even in 1 *Kaḷā*, there was still all the beauty that one can imagine and *Sañkalps* still had the power to create. So if you look at it positively, though the ratio of *Paṛam Tatva* was just 6 to 10 per cent the place inhabited was still paradise when compared to our physical world. This means that if we really are serious, and meditate and affirm, in a more disciplined and selfless manner, then we can ascend to this level and create a world which is so many times more blissful and pure than our materialistic world. Yes, it would be an infant stage of the soul, moving towards the immortal elements.

"Now we reach 0 Celestial Degree or Zero *Kaḷā* which is our present world with five elements where we are almost left with negligible *Paṛam Tatva* that help us to survive here. Right now the earth which we inhabit is in a negative stage; this in reality is not even the stage of 0 Celestial Degree. We are still moving below and below, but for referral point reasons, we say that this is Zero *Kaḷā*." Concluded *Sakshi*.

"*Betā* you must understand that when we started to descend, the three elements started to increase and because of the three elements, a particular heaviness entered into the *Tatva*. And since the *Paṛam* light vanished, the *Paṛam Tatva* too started to diminish and the *Gross Tatva* began to rule." Informed *Bapuji*. "In Zero *Kaḷā*, there are heavy elements and we are ruled by five elements which are getting heavier and heavier. Take the *Vāyu Tatva* as an example. In air itself we have hydrogen, oxygen etc. etc. adding up to so many different elements or *Vāyus*. Now we say *Dhàṛti Tatva*, then how many elements are there in Mother Earth itself? There is iron, marble, gold, silver, so on and so forth. Thus the heaviness increased tremendously in the five elements. Each soul has a subtle body. And the subtle body has its origin and environment from where it has come about. And since each person's thoughts are different, the subtle body of each will be different and thus his or her place of origin is also different. In fact each and every *Brahṁāṇḍ* or creation is different.

"Now when a human soul commits a lot of sins or goes away from the Light, the soul's energy goes down. Going away from the Light and sinning means the soul will lose its power. Now where are all the Karmas recorded? They are stored in the soul. When Karmas recorded in the soul have more sins then the individual's subtle body gets affected. The subtle and astral bodies too get weak. Our physical body has many other bodies within it. Inside the physical gross body, is the subtle body, i.e. the three-elemental body... Then inside that is the *Kāṛaṇ Śarēr* which we call the reason or Causal body. This Causal body refers to the body whose *raison d'être* is the accumulated effect of all our words, thoughts and deeds since the beginning of the soul's journey.

"So the *Sūkśṃ* body is made of three elements and inside the astral or *Sūkśṃ* body is the Causal body. The Causal body is made of two elements, Light and Space. There is no element of Air or Wind in the Causal body. The *Kāṛaṇsaṛi* or reason of being of the *Kāṛaṇ Śarēr* is the collective negative or positive *Sañkalps* or intentions and desires. The Causal body or *Kāṛaṇ Śarēr* is typically effected by the *Ākāś Taŧva* or the silence or the lack of it, within.

"Now what is not mentioned is that, there is a body beyond the Causal body too and that is called the *Māhā Kāṛaṇ* or Most Subtle Causal body or the Causal of the Causal. The *Māhā* Causal body is made only of the *Ākāś Taŧva*. Only silence. And all these bodies make us a complete individualistic identity in all of creation. As you go higher up, you go into the *Māhā Causal* body made only of the *Ākāś Taŧva*. And if you reach a point where once again the *Paṛam Taŧva* or the Prime Elements enter your Causal body composition, even by one per cent in the *Ākāś Taŧva*, then you immediately reach *Brahṁāpuri* that is the 8th Dimension of heaven. And if the *Paṛam Taŧva* increase by four per cent then you reach *Viśnupuri*, the 9th Dimension; but to go to *Viśnupuri* you have to work really, really hard. And to go from *Viśnupuri* to *Śivpuri* that is the 10th Dimension, one needs five and more per cent of *Paṛam Taŧvas* in the *Māhā Causal* body."

Thus eventually one will have in the *Māhā Causal* body the *Ākāś Taŧva*, *Paṛam Taŧva* and then logically the *Māhā Taŧva* and the last stage just *Paṛam Pṛakāś*. But eventually it all starts with selfless love and wanting peace, joy, laughter, wellbeing for all of creation.

15

It was late November and the next day we were to leave for *Pune*. The morning newspapers announced that for the past twenty-odd years, this month in Delhi had not experienced such a freezing winter! *Meher* and I were still tucked in bed. We were watching this cartoon *Chotta Bheem.* It is about a boy with a bunch of friends and this boy, once he eats *laḍoos* (a sweetmeat), gets exceptional strength and wallops all and sundry to smithereens. Those days this cartoon was all we watched and I myself had seen them so often that I wished I could have added something else in the *laḍoos* to put an end to *Chotta Bheem* and my misery.

"You see Daddy you have to eat those *laḍoos* to become as strong as *Chotta Bheem*."

"Honey, if I start to eat those *laḍoos* like that neurotic friend of yours, I will have cholesterol detected even in my family jewels!"

"Daddy not good, not good, this is not the way to talk to your daughter…! And he eats these *laḍoos* because he gets magical powers…! He becomes very strong… very, very strong!"

"And what a missed opportunity to instil in crazy kids like you – the knowledge of the power of prayers; that prayers can give one immense strength. But instead, this half-clad boy gets his magical strength eating *laḍoos*! What a beautiful opportunity to make kids move towards God and one's Master but no, now they will move towards *laḍoos*."

"Daddy if you pray before eating even a *laḍoo na*, saying that *Sai Bābā* and *Mā*, please come eat with me and bless me, then that is good enough. And will you shave your beard it is poking me when you kiss me… hee… hee! *Chotta Bheem* savings me from this bearded *rākśas* of a Daddy! And you are again going to that *Bapuji*…!" She snorted. "I hate this hotel, horrible place, there's no mall over here… and I hope *Bapuji* is not going to come with us to *Pune*. I am very upset with him and… you are an idiot Daddy, why *doos* you have to write books? *Doos* I write books… no *na*?! There are many people who can write books. Let them. Nobody reads books. Do I read books? No. Why? Because you *keeps* telling me *na*… that television is more interesting than human *deings*…"

"Human beings… not *deings*..."

"Don't goes to *Bapuji* today. Stays with me or send mummy."

"My love, *Bapuji* is not too well! Let us say your mother's aura will overwhelm him..."

She chuckled and realized that she wasn't sticking to the script.

"Stupid Delhi and this hotel and this *Bapuji* and I hate you Daddy."

After an hour I sat in the car, made sure the heater was on full blast, felt myself begin to defrost, and shut my eyes. Why couldn't God just maintain the temperature at one rational level? Not too hot or cold. Why create diverse climates? Just create one moderate climate and be done with! But no…, He had to go about creating. If only He had not created the stomach to be elastic and expandable, there wouldn't be hunger in the world or the innumerable issues that come about with the lack of food or the gluttony over food. What was He smoking when He went about scripting this extremely horror-of-a-plot called life…?

I was back with *Mataji*. Both, *Anant* and *Sakshi* had left for *Ahmedabad*. After sipping on some hot coffee, I switched on the Dictaphone.

"Does *Bapuji* have a Guru?"

"*Betā*, the Guru of *Bapuji* is 'The One Up Above' or as he says, '*Uparwālā*'. There is surely someone up there who is the Guru of *Bapuji*. *Bapuji's Paṛam, Paṛam Satya Guru* or the Beyond-the-Beyond Master who is even beyond the Ethereal element of yonder and many times beyond the yonder there is one just like *Bapuji*. It is his *Swarūp* or his Divine *Avatār* made of the Supreme Light.

"That is why at once the *Swarūp* is *Nirākāri*, *Ākāri* and *Sākāri* which means without form, in spirit form and with a physical form. That same *Swarūp* or Divine Form does what it wants to do from and through *Bapuji*. That *Swarūp* created its Own *Rūp* or Image or Clone and sent it to the *Sākār* or the physical world or the World of Forms, to do what must be done. To try and give knowledge to one and all, that we all can move beyond the physical and bring about joy, peace, eternal happiness and wellbeing through all of creation.

"So *Bapuji's* Guru is His *Avyăkt Swarūp*, or His Subtle Self or His Higher Self. That Self sends the knowledge and the experience to *Bapuji* in his physical form. The main message that needs to be passed forth is that 'when the Light of that Power House or The Great Flame will get pulled down to earth through *Yog* or meditation, that is when the *Amar Taŧva* or the Eternal Elements which is another word for *Paṛam Taŧva or* Prime Elements will be brought down to earth."

Ok, so my sweet intellectually confounded, bordering on the profane… sorry…, profound reader of mine! Basically, the way this is going to happen, as I have understood, is that in reality, this bringing down of the prime elements, isn't the job or the sole prerogative of one particular man, child or woman. This is going to be possible, when as a group or as a whole, we all work together towards manifesting the Prime Elements or *Paṛam Taṫvas*, down on to Mother Earth by sending the right affirmations and praying for peace and happiness for all of creation.

How is this going to happen? Smart question *Raaabert*! It is going to happen by first going beyond the body. This means by not identifying yourself only with the body, but identifying with the spirit (and I don't mean the brand or type of alcohol consumed) within you and realizing that 'I am the spirit in this body and I am not the body but the spirit that is housed in this body'. This is the first and the most important step, and only when you are completely convinced and clear in your Conscious, Sub-Conscious, and Auric-Consciousness (this is my term for referring to all the emotions and patterns stored in the astral and causal bodies), that you are the spirit and not the body, only then will you be able to truly create your *Avatār* or *Rūp* or satellite, that shall be able to bring forth not only the *Paṛam Taṫva* or The Prime Elements, the *Māhā Taṫva* or the Divine Light but even *Paṛam Pṛakāś* that is Supreme Divine Radiance and through affirmations of pure joy, peace, happiness, divinity and wellbeing create paradise not only for mankind but for all of creation.

"Isn't all this what our soul really craves for; craves for the Supreme Authority, the Almighty Authority, the Light House and the Power House. There exists energy, '*Ātmā ka Taṫva*', which is an Element of the Soul. And as desires keep increasing the power of the soul diminishes, and due to this the body and the atmosphere both become weak. The five elements too turn frail. Now in this world there are many instruments of pleasure that are made, but man doesn't know that it is these that are the cause of pain and sorrow. And that is why let us all together through the

Yog Jñān or Meditative Knowledge, bring down the *Amrut Tatva* or the Divine Elements onto the earth.

"Everyone has different Gurus. But the importance of the *Paṛam Satya Guru* or the Supreme Primordial Master is beyond everything and all others. The *Paṛam Satya Guru* can only be One. *Paṛam* means the Supreme, the Greatest or the Prime. I believe that the duty of the *Paṛam Satya Guru* is to make us all Supreme. So how will we search for this *Paṛam Satya Guru*? The Primordial Master is that One who will give us knowledge and through knowledge liberate us and set us free from all bondage, including the bondage with the lower self. Everybody has his or her philosophy but the Supreme Master will reveal the *Paṛam Satya Jñān* or the Supreme Knowledge of Truth and set us all free. That One only can be…the *Paṛam Satya Guru*. He and only He can liberate us from the clutches of *Kāḷ* or Time. Today for most human beings the biggest fear is that of death."

I often feel it may not be the fear of one's own mortality or death but the death or passing over of one's loved ones which is the greatest fear. One's own death or passing over is for many the greatest liberation. For countless people life is just another four letter word and thus death is a release but the passing over of a loved one, could be the greatest fear.

"Now how does one get free from death? How can one get free from the jaws of death? That knowledge the *Paṛam Satya Guru* will impart and He will give us techniques to attain a body of the *Amar Tatva* or the Supreme Elements. He will tell us how one can break free from the clutches of Time. How one can be *Akāl Mooṛt* or a Form Free From All Death, where Time or *Kāḷ* cannot gobble you up and thus make you *Akāl Puṛakh* or Timeless and Forever? How does one go to *Amar Lok* or the Immortal World and not the *Mṛutyu Lok* that is the World of Death? How does one reach the world where there is no birth or death, and be free from the world of the five elements? If you belong to a world of the five elements, then death is imminent. You will keep coming back innumerable times.

"What knowledge will the *Paṛam Satya Guru* impart? What powers does He have? He will give us knowledge and teach such *Yog* that our body will convert into the Supreme Elements with the practice of *Yog* even while on earth. And the complete universe will be given the knowledge of being set free from the clutches of death. The One who has the power to convert the impossible to the possible and show us the way to become one with the Supreme Light is the Primordial Guru. With this body only, through the practice of *Yog*, the Primordial Master will impart to us the ancient knowledge to become *Amar* or Immortal or be in the state of Forever.

"The *Paṛam Satya Guru* of us all is the *Viśwa* Guru or the World Mentor who can only be One and He can come through in any form and through different forms. He is pure Energy. He is simple. Will look like a normal man and behaves like a normal man but one needs to go beyond the façade of normalcy and see His Divinity. The One who imparts this knowledge of liberating oneself from the cycle of life and death and teaches the *Yog* or technique of reaching The Supreme Abode, that One only is the *Viśwa Guru* or the Master of the World.

"I have been asked time and again why we refer to the *Vedas* or the *Puṛāṇas* or the various Hindu *Śāstṛās* to share our knowledge and does that mean that only what is in these Holy Scriptures followed by the Hindus is the final referral point. No. Each ancient Text talks the same thing. *Bapuji* takes the support of these Scriptures to explain his knowledge to people, so it will be understood easily.

"I remember talking to *Bapuji* about when exactly did his journey really begin? As he has told you, as a child itself, he always wondered how the world, the moon, the stars, the sun, etc, whatever he could see with his eyes, was created. He had to focus on his professional life and his family. He did not come from affluence. He had to work hard and take care of his family. But as he often tells me, his mind would continually ruminate about these essential spiritual questions. Wherever he went and he met men of God, he would inquire and most often he was never really satisfied with the answers he got. On January 1st 1996, he saw his own *Swarūp,* his Divine Image. He watched himself and told us later that, 'I was up there and I was down here too. Just like this five-elemental body here, there is another *Swarūp* up there as well!' And this experience came to him after decades of searching for The One. Long after *Bapuji's* marriage and children and professional life, he was given this vision and the reason being, he never ever gave up on asking the right questions from the Creator and his thirst for knowledge and self realization eventually was rewarded with the vision.

"Remember *betā,* this knowledge that he has shared with us, even the *Śāstṛās* have not revealed. There is a wee-bit, a miniscule amount of what he has divulged in what's found in the Holy Books. But the complete knowledge he has divulged through his own personal experiences and imparted to a few and now through you and your book it will be available to all the true seekers. This is not about Hinduism. This is universal knowledge.

"You have asked me what is the Golden Rule to go beyond the limited into the beyond the beyond? The fact of the matter is that we can cross the finite and go to the beyond the beyond initially with our *Buđhi* or mind and intellect. Because so high-up and above no machine or vehicle can ever reach or take you but the mind can take you anywhere. The world was created by The Original Whim or Thought. To reach the Golden Energy, the vast distance cannot be covered any other way than by the instrument it was created with and that is the Mind. There is no one who can reach there. But our Intellect or *Buđhi* can take one to any place, anywhere, at anytime.

"The best way to go about this process is to spare some time from your busy schedule each day and take your spirit body high up there. You will first do it with your mind, but after a while, you will realize that you truly are moving up there and after a while living up there in the causal body. Take your *Swarūp* or Divine Self beyond the five elements, beyond our galaxy, beyond the beyond, as that is the place you have to travel to reach the Supreme Abode. Keep at it. Just keep at it. You will realize what *Bapuji* has experienced. You can continue to live your normal life in the five elements and also in the Divine Image. And when these Energies come into us our *Sañkalps* or thoughts and desires become less, our *Mun* – that is our heart becomes silent and peaceful. Our *Moh* that is our attachment gets destroyed. Our desires reduce to a bare minimum and our mind becomes less cluttered till a stage comes when you are in the moment.

"But how far will one grow depends upon the individual's fervour for spiritual attainment and liberation. The more fervent one's desire to be free from karmic bondage, the faster the spiritual growth of the person... If you want to run the marathon, one has to be truly dedicated and keep building one's stamina and pace. Your book *The Last Marathon* too says the same thing. Liberation is the last marathon. There has to be a single-minded pursuit to start-off with and with complete dedication, slowly you will reach your destination. Our soul's energy is virtually finished and that is why the body's power too is weak. Thousands of years back our body had the power to change form and again go back to the Light Form. That is because the soul hạd that kind of power due to the purity in the elements. So take yourself to a place where the elements are Supreme and you will be able to infuse your soul with immense energy and through your soul your body too will feel the immense energy. That is why I truly believe your book will make all the difference. Not many will be able to come and get this knowledge from the source; *Bapuji.* Thus your book will be the medium and the path to show countless seekers the way to liberation and bring about positive change in all of creation. The book will teach the seeker to go beyond the five elements, to go where there is Supreme Divine Radiance, *Paṛam Pṛakāś* and absorb this Supreme Divine Radiance which exists many times further away from even the *Ākāś Taṫva* that is the element of Ether or Space. If our intellect can reach there, then we can absorb this Divine Radiance, and spread it to all of creation.

"Our knowledge that we have imparted is so simple, and yet, one can become so powerful without the support of anyone; once the Light and *Śakti* comes into us, then we become powerful and *Nih-Sañkalp* or without selfish desires and thoughts. When you attain such power, you will not speak much with anyone, nor will you have an urge to roam about here and there. You will remain in silence. The energy of silence will enter into you. This is a sure sign that the Divine Power has begun to increase within you. This will become a core characteristic of your personality. In that soul, these energies will enter. Then you will try to delve deeper into the ocean of knowledge. You will try to go into the depth of silence and you will try to unearth the very beginning, the middle and the end of creation; by knowing creation you will know the Creator better and knowing the Creator better you will know yourself more clearly and most importantly through you, the world will benefit from this *Yog*, as you will only desire the wellbeing, joy and peace for all of creation. What more can you ask for from life or the Creator?"

True. To desire to bring about *Sukh* and *Śañti*

(Happiness and Peace) in all of creation, is the most noble of all intentions.

Throughout our conversation there was mention of *Brahmakumaris*. Was there an over-lapping of philosophy? I was curious as the last thing one wants is a controversy especially when one doesn't need a controversy to put across a point of view. So I inquired with *Mataji* regarding the similarity between *Bapuji*'s philosophy and that believed by *Brahmakumaris.* I needed to hear it and it was important I wrote about it. So bear with me.

"We went to the *Brahmakumari Sanstha,* and I heard their philosophy as well. Those days I had not yet met *Bapuji,* and my search was still on. The *Brahmakumari* philosophy is very sound and their belief systems and concepts are very good. They impart good knowledge. One attains peace as well. But they claim that the world drama is just 5000 years old. This complete creation of the world or nature or *Sṛuśti Chakra* is as recent as 5000 years. So according to them the state of *Swarg* or heaven is just before 5000 years. Now spiritually or even scientifically this doesn't make sense. This bit we were unable to understand from the start.

"The *Agatya Vāṇis* or the Subtle Voice of the Cosmos that keeps flowing cannot just be as recent as 5000 years old. They say that the *Vāṇis* keep on flowing and they flow with the Grace of God. We completely agree with this concept and through this flow of the Subtle Voice we get the *Māhā Vakyās* or phrases and sentences containing profound wisdom. These *Māhā Vakyās* reveal profound truths and wisdom through the *Manañ* and *Chintan* or deep meditation and contemplation upon them. That is why we read their *Vāṇis.* We do not deem any *Sanstha* or association wrong. But we give the knowledge of the Beyond the Beyond the innumerable trillion *Brāhmāṇḍs*.

"The claim that on this earth 5000 years ago there was *Swarg* or heaven prevailed just doesn't make sense. They say that in *Swarg* or heaven peace and happiness prevailed. Sure. True. In heaven one would expect only peace and happiness to prevail. But our contention is that if a *Swarg* or heaven-like state prevailed, why did so many battles and wars rage 5000 years before? How could fights, quarrels, pettiness and wars take place in *Swarg*? The incidence of *Māhābhāṛăta* is said to have occurred 5000 years or before; whoever knows anything about the *Māhābhāṛăta* knows that there was immense politics and bloodshed that took place during that time. How can one claim that bloodshed and war and politics took place in *Swarg?* In heaven, first and foremost the body is not made-up of the five elements at all! If you read the *Māhābhāṛăta* it was all about five-elemental issues. If you were to read world history, or books on creation, you would know that 5000 years is nothing when compared to the state of slow evolution that this universe has gone through and our galaxy and planet has undergone. To claim that 5000 years ago one was in a state of paradise is wishful thinking.

"When in *Swarg* or heaven or in that state of spiritual advancement, first of all the body is made up of *Māhā Tatva* or just Pure Divine Light. Why would people wage war when encased in Pure Divine Light? So this is where our ideologies do not meet. They also claim that *Bhagwan Śiva Bābā* or Lord *Śiva* is present on Earth now. So where is He and how is He? What knowledge is He imparting? How is the world still in such a state of flux? Till now no one has really answered these questions. That is why we would go to the *Sanstha* with great love, listen to them, understand them and there are some really good ideologies on purity that they teach. A lot of what is taught there is priceless. But the fundamental point that our world began 5000 years ago, the way we know it, is unacceptable. We give the knowledge of Beyond the Innumerable Trillions of *Brähmāṇḍs*. We give knowledge that is beyond the *Anant*

Koti Brähmāñḍs. We also believe in what the scientific world through its research is imparting. We also believe in a bit of the knowledge that the *Śāstṛās* have given us, whereas they do not even believe in the *Śāstṛās*. They say that the *Śāstṛās* are untrue, do not read them.

"Thus the basic difference between the *Brahmakumaris* and us is that they claim that the *Sṛuśti Chakra* or creation is 5000 years old and that our *Śāstṛās* are untrue. We refuse to accept this. They have divided the 5000 years into four parts. And they say that the soul takes birth 84 times. Even if you start to calculate, you will be unable to get the math right. So the 5000-year-long *Sṛuśti Chakra* cannot be right at all. *Śrī Ram* came much before Lord *Kṛiṣna*. Lord *Kṛiṣna* itself was on earth 5000 years ago. *Śrī Ram* was much before Lord *Kṛiṣna; Shañkarji*, the father of Lord *Gaṇeśa* and Lord *Kāṛtikeya* came much, much before *Śrī Ram*. These incidents have taken place thousands of years ago. So how can we believe in the theory dated only 5000 years ago? The *Brahmakumaris* claim that *Sat Yug* is just 1250 years and *Kal Yug* is 1250 hundred years and between are the other two *Yugs*. According to *Bapuji, Sat Yug* is 17,27000 human years. *Treytā Yug* is 12,16,000 human years. *Dvāpar Yug* is 8,64,000 human years and *Kal Yug* is 4,32,000 human years. Thus one cycle of creation is called *Chatur Yug* which is 46,20,000 human years. Now compare it to just 5000 years that they claim."

You know what, if you ask me, get beyond all this too. Just focus on giving your Master and life a hundred per cent. Give of yourself to spread Light, share of your abundance or even whatever little one has. Try to spread joy and happiness but more importantly don't spread unhappiness and strife and negativity. Life sometimes can get overwhelming. Those times know just one thing, your Master is with you and together the tough times will pass too. Just keep your focus on trying to give your level best to life and every moment. Be cool. Be calm. Good and bad times will come and pass. Stay centered. Know you are special as the cosmos has invested all its resources in creating you. How does it matter how old is our creation? Who gives a rat's arse? Does it feed a hungry child, or clothed a naked baby? How does it matter how everything was created? Just focus on being centered and trying to help somebody who needs help. All ideologies on one hand and feeding a hungry child on the other, I will go and feed the hungry child. May be I won't get liberation; tough blasted luck. The only thing I want liberation is from my own lower/limited/imperfect/incomplete/petty/inferior/mediocre/insignificant, other self.

Heaven and hell don't even come into the picture.

Neither does God or the demon.

16

I sat with *Bapuji*. This was the last time we would sit together for the book. I really didn't know when we would meet again.

"*Beta* what is this state of *Samadhi* or Liberation that everybody keeps talking about? The state of *Samadhi* according to me means the real state of the Soul. When an individual recognizes one's true state, it gains knowledge of the Self or the *Ātma-Jñān* or knowledge of the soul. To attain the *Samadhi Avastha*, what does the soul have to do? What kind of a *Purusharth* or appropriate action does the soul have to perform? Whatever recording the soul has within itself, all that knowledge the soul will gain. Every soul is different in that it may be of 9 *Kala* or 10 *Kala* or even16 *Kala* or a soul may even belong to the *Bayhuđ Ka Paṛam Dhām* or the Prime Abode, while another may be a *Paṛam, Paṛam, Paṛam Ātmā*, the Supreme, Supreme, Supreme Soul. Basically the *Paṛam Pitā* or the Founding Father of the Infinite is One only and thus the *Paṛam Ātmā* or Founding Soul is also just One.

"One can go into the *Samadhi* State only after following certain procedures, mainly celibacy and yogic breathing. Unless one does not achieve that level of *Brāhṁācharya* or celibacy, one cannot achieve *Samadhi*. They say that if one keeps untainted celibacy for twelve long years and such a person is celibate even in the state of dreams and keeps his or her celibacy intact for twelve years and that person also practices *Pṛāṇāyam* or yogic breathing everyday and does the chant of the sacred word *Aum*, he or she will awaken the power of the soul, which reposes in the root chakra or the *Muladhār Chakra*. When the *Muladhār Chakra* gets awakened, the energy travels through the other *Chakras* and reaches the soul."

Wow! Celibacy and *Prāṇāyam* for twelve years; I think it is safe to say most of us are going to be in the state of non-*Samadhi* for a realllllllllllly longgggggggg time!

But to tell you the truth, I don't believe that celibacy has anything got to do with spirituality or even *Samadhi*. Yes, celibacy helps if you are keen on awakening your *Kundalini* and want to acquire certain paranormal powers. In sex, the very word 'discharge', means, something that once had power, through dissipation of energy, the power has got discharged.

So if you are keen on taking the energy that reposes in the *Muladhār Chakra*, (also known as the root Chakra), and make the *Kundalini Śakti* travel through the other *Chakras*, right up to the Crown *Chakra*, then yes, it is important that the energy is not discharged via sexual release. But that is if you want to acquire powers or *Siđhis*. But to be spiritual, I believe the power of God, reposes in the Heart *Chakra*, which is well above the naughty *Chakra*, and thus by being selfless, pure, kind, noble (not stupid, just noble), you will merge with your Master, with or without the use of the libido. God's kingdom is not filled with celibates. It is filled with good people. Heaven is not some exclusive club for vegetarians and celibates. It's packed with honest to God, fun loving, kind hearted, souls, who wish well, and who want to spread wellbeing.

"Just for intellectual reasons, where does the soul reside?" I inquired. *Bapuji* had a broad grin on his face and a twinkle in his eyes.

"In the third eye or *Ājña Chakra*, between the eyebrows, resides the soul; the point in between the brows on the forehead. When one does *Anulom* and *Vilom* or alternative nostril breathing as practiced in Yogic *Prāṇāyam*, the entire subtle body comes together at one place that is in the centre point between the brows. Thus, through the practice of celibacy and yogic breathing, the soul remembers its *Ishta Dev* or one's Primordial God, Goddess or Guru; basically the One he or she prays to, which could be the family deity, or a *Devi* or *Devatā* or the *Paṛam Brāhṁā Parameśwar*, or the formless *Śiva* or *Śiva* with a form or one's Guru. Thus, while doing yogic breathing or *Prāṇāyam* one needs to focus on the One who you believe in and worship. So by performing the *Prāṇāyam* or *Anulom – Vilom*, and the chanting of the *Aum* sound, all the subtle energies gather into the soul and the soul awakens. That is when the soul experiences the subtle mind and goes into complete silence and the *Nih-Sañkalp Avastha* or State of Formlessness. Focus on your God or Goddess or Guru, and make sure your mind doesn't stray. After a while your mind will be truly focused. It will not be able to see anything else and will be able to see only that, and only that, and only that... And by focusing on the yogic breathing and on your *Ishta Devatā*, whatever power that *Ishta Devatā* will have, will get transferred to you. Thus, be careful who you keep your focus on during meditation and *Prāṇāyam*.

"So, when the complete subtle body converges into the soul, the lack of a subtle body within the gross body leaves a vacuum and there is no consciousness of the body. So then the soul reaches the *Sahastrāgār*; the 9th Chakra. (This I assume is in the astral body of each individual as the crown *Chakra* is the seventh *Chakra*.) In the *Sahastrāgār*, there is the cell of each soul's *Rachanas* or creations. In the *Sahastrāgār* there is the *Brāhṁāñḍ*. There are cells of the *Anant Koti Brāhṁāñḍs* or innumerable crores of creations. So in the *Samadhi* state, the soul experiences the recordings that are already there in the soul and gains Self or Soul Knowledge. So whatever recording is present in the soul, the individual gets to know of that and as the soul has come from far and above, the knowledge is enlightening.

"The soul's state will be in the *Samadhi Avastha* or State of Liberation when there is no body consciousness. That is why *Gautam Buddha* sometimes could not hear any sound, even if you hammered a nail into His ear... that is the State of *Samadhi*. So when the subtle mind opens up, that is what I call as the state of *Samadhi*. By staying in the subtle… or one can even call this state the Prime Sub-Conscious Mind, the soul becomes totally awakened to its history and potential. There is so much of silence that someone who looks at the individual will assume the person is dead. The more you move into this state of *Samadhi,* the soul of that person comes out of the body along with its subtle body. How does this happen? The *Dasam Dwār* or the tenth door or the 10th *Chakra* opens. So when the soul comes out it goes away to roam into its *Brāhṁāñḍ* or its creation. So where does the soul really go? It can go to the *Bhu Lok, Bhubhrū Lok, Jan Lok, Tap Lok,* basically the various levels of heaven. And if it has more power then it can travel up to *Brāhṁāpuri,* and if the power is even more, it can travel up to *Viśnupuri* as well. It will never desire to go below into the levels of hell or *Pātāl Lok.*

"And the souls with the capacity of the *Māhā Śiva,* those can travel up to the *Māhā Brāhṁāñḍ,* it can go to the Infinite *Koti Brāhṁāñḍs.* Souls in the capacity of *Paṛam Māhā Śiva* can travel up to the *Paṛam Māhā Brāhṁāñḍ* and up to the bigger and brighter suns. Because its body is made of *Ākāś Tatva* or Ether or Space Element, it finally turns into that element. Its body is just made of the *Ākāś Tatva.*

"When the soul's body is made of the *Vāyu Tatva* or Wind element, it is called *Manomay Sharēr* or the body of the mind and heart, which means that it can travel with the speed of thought or as per the speed of the *Mun* or desire, which is many times faster than the speed of light. So for instance if it has to travel from one galaxy to another, then it would take not more than a moment. Because it is the speed of the *Mun;* one thought and it is there! It can travel far and wide through the galaxies, the *Māhā* galaxies, five lakh light years away, ten lakh light years away, and even one-crore or trillion light years away, but only if it has the *Paṛam Paṛam Paṛam Māhā* capacity only then can it travel so far, otherwise the soul of this *Brähṁāñḍ* cannot travel out of this *Brähṁāñḍ*, and the *Māhā Brähṁāñḍ's* soul can go up to the *Māhā Brähṁāñḍ*. Thus, even the soul has its limitations according to its recordings. You have the evolved soul; the very evolved soul; the very, very evolved soul and so on and so forth.

"But no one can travel beyond the 1.5 trillion light years, because there is a limiting circumference or circular limit that is beyond the 1.5 trillion light years and it is all sealed. So beyond that no one can ever go even if it is the *Paṛam Pitā* or Founding Father of the Infinite, even though the *Paṛam Pitā* has created the *Paṛam Ātmās* or Prime Souls, He is still not the Almighty Authority. The Almighty Authority who is the Infinite or *Para-Brähṁ-Parameśwar*, created the first of creation, the earliest and first creation which is the *Paṛam Pitā* or Founding Father of the Infinite. The Founding Father created the *Paṛam Ātmās* or Prime Souls and then the *Paṛam Ātmās* created the *Dev-Ātmās* or God like Souls and *Dev-Ātmās* then created the human souls.

"If you go into the Subtle or Prime Sub Conscious Mind then you will go beyond the limited mind and you will go beyond the limited bodily relations or blood relations as well. You cannot remember anything related to your daily life when you are at that stage. From the Subtle or Prime Sub Conscious you reach the Prime Unconscious Mind. You are part of the process of creation. So much energy comes into the soul that you get the speed of the Infinite *Mun* or the Heart-Mind called, *'Bayhuḋ Kay Mun Ki Gati'* or

Speed of Infinite Heart-Mind. There is so much speed as there is so much power.

"But, today why are the souls entangled? Why is the state of *Samadhi* not so easily reachable? Tell me *betā*?"

"Is that a trick question? I mean twelve years of celibacy and go about life doing alternate nostril breathing, I mean, come on. There has to be a better way to tap into ones subtle or pure sub consciousness?"

When *Bapuji* laughs his eyes twinkle like that of a child.

"Naughty boy you are. The reason the state of *Samadhi* is so elusive is because we are all entangled into body consciousness and involved in the body and entangled in everything that is related with the body and our circle of emotions. So most people see the body and then remember only the body. They immediately come into body consciousness and the whole game is over. What can one do? That is why awakening the pure subconscious mind is so important. One can call the awakening of the subtle mind as a state of 'enlightened death' too. The soul goes into such a state of calm silence that we refer to it as death. The process removes the subtle body out and allows the soul to move out of the body. Many of our *Rūśimunis* or evolved Sages had the knowledge of going out of the body at will. They would travel, gather consciously all knowledge they wanted and then try to enlighten the world."

According to me the more you get into the technicalities of spirituality the more you realize that heaven and hell are within each of us; the blossoming of one's true self and the destruction of all that which is true; all within oneself. The power to discriminate between right and wrong and the power to choose between the Light or the chaos within, all in our own within. For me liberation means being free from one's own clutches of darkness and desires and shedding off of the false self and letting one's true self shine through. And it is not easy. The path to liberating yourself from your lower self is filled with spiritual landmines and failure. But you just keep at it. Fall. Rise. Fall. Rise. Keep at it. Try and try and try to lengthen the moments of Light and prolong the distance between the moments of darkness. Yes, we are human and yes, we are going to blunder and so we need try harder to embrace the Light for a little longer. The Light within is elusive; it's playful; it's a lover who wants to be possessed but won't ever surrender till you are worthy, so you keep at it and someday, may be lifetimes later, you and I and *Laloo Prasad Yadav*, will be worthy of Her and be filled with Her and radiate Her essence and then become one with Her. Just keep at it. Trying to make one's Master happy and proud of you, in spite of falling so many times is the only dream worth having and till you don't reach it, keep trying and trying. That is the only true purpose of life.

Raising the *Kundalini* and *Nirvāna* and all that is super, but as *Sai Bābā of Shirdi* often says, there is a difference between *Siđhī* and *Shuđhi* which means there is a difference between spiritual powers and spiritual purity. You may have your *Kundalini* all awakened and suited and booted, but that gives no guarantee of true spiritual growth. But yearning to be spiritually pure has one guarantee; it's going to tickle the Old Man's funny bone and make Him grin, from one astral ear to the other.

That for me is worth more than all the *Brāhṁāñḍs* in all the universes.

17

This book has been quite a journey. Since I began my research for the book until its completion, a lot has transpired. There has been a dramatic shift in the process of channeling. A Braille version of *The Fakir* reached all the libraries for those who are visually challenged. *Meher* has begun liking movies that feature *Akshay Kumar* and *Salman Khan*, especially for their soul stirring dialogues and heartwarming dances and songs and by the way, she got first prize doing her version of ballet, the sweetest three minutes of my life, seeing her on stage. And yes, mercifully we keep watching cartoons that feature our real Rock Stars like *Śṛi Ram, Sita Mā,* Lord *Hanuman,* Lord *Kṛiśna,* Lord *Balram* and of course *Chotta Bheem,* who for some reason continues to eat those *ladoos* without any seemingly harmful ramifications on his cholesterol or fat level in his body.

On this journey of writing this book there are a few by-lanes that I thought I would revisit and further elaborate.

In this book a lot is spoken about *Ākāsh Tatva*. The element of ether or void or space or silence and it is important to understand the essence of silence which we are referring to. Please note that the silence that is being referred to is the silence within oneself. Silence is of utmost importance but it is the silence within that is of supreme significance. The silence that emanates from the very depth of one's soul and like a soft breeze, carrying the fragrance of spring, spreads through one's being, one's consciousness and one's very breath. It is the silence of being in the moment. It is the sound of peace. It is the rhythm of calm and positive acceptance. It is the beginning of the true state of nothingness. But that doesn't mean you stop feeling, or speaking, or thinking or contemplating. It only means you decide when to speak, think, contemplate and even worry. There is a time you allocate for everything, and in between those slots there is just calm nothingness.

The reason I am going on and on about silence is that a few years ago, during a session of channeling, a very close friend of mine, had been advised to become more silent, as he was going through certain issues, where fate and life, had sort of made him lie down, flat on the ground, spread his legs, and with spiked shoes, were jumping on his family jewels. So *Bābā Sai of Shirdi* had advised him to go within, find his zone of peace and silence, stay there, till the tide turned in favour of him and things got back to normal.

A few weeks later I got a call from his dangerous half.

"You told my husband, your friend, to be silent?" Her tone should have warned me about her mood but I have gone about life with little regard for personal safety, thus I passed a comment, which I shouldn't have.

"That is not funny *Ruzbeh,* your opinion about wives in general, and women in particular, speaks of a very troubled childhood."

"What nonsense, as a child I thought women were from planet earth and the best thing to have happened to mankind. Just goes to show how innocent we are as children."

I heard, what sounded like the snort of a really disgruntled bull.

"I have called to say whatever you have told my demented husband isn't working. The bastard has stopped talking to everybody. He only nods his fat head and gives a goofy smile that makes me want to disembowel him. I am putting the phone in his hand. Talk him out of whatever you have got him into or else I know where you live."

What had transpired was that my friend, had taken this going into silence, a little too literally, and had stopped speaking to one and all. This isn't the silence we are talking about. The silence is a state of mind. Where there is a state of acceptance. The level of wants, thoughts, desires, restlessness, is controlled or curtailed, to the best of one's capabilities. It's not about just talking less it's about wanting less, and being less in the state of angst. It's the silence of the mind and heart, rather than just of the tongue.

The second point I want to make clear is that there is nothing wrong when one prays to one's God, Goddess or Master, directing one's love and devotion to a statue or a photograph. It is foolhardy to expect the photograph or statue of one's Supreme One, to talk back or come to life. If you believe that God resides in everything and everyone, why is it so difficult to believe, that the Supreme One, resides in a statue or a photograph. We are simple people, who need a form or an image, to concentrate our love and devotion. So don't go about disregarding your love for your Supreme One, just because you pray to a photograph or statue. You are praying to the Supreme One, using the snap or statue, to focus your love and attention. There is nothing wrong. If you truly pray with all your love and devotion, you will see even the photograph or statue of your Supreme One, respond back; smile at you, love you, be a little upset, console you, warm your very being. There are various ways to express love and devotion to one's loved One, and if you need a form or an image, so be it. Just don't get fanatical about your love for the Supreme One. Don't get judgmental about somebody else's faith and love. Live and let live. God is about love and laughter.

Not about hate and discrimination. If you can see your Supreme One in a snap or a statue and not see Him or Her in another living being, then there is a problem. Something has gone wrong. Otherwise, all is well. It is Oneness that is going to open the doors of your higher self and clear your path for your spiritual growth. Only the firm affirmation and belief is needed, that we all are One and have come from the One. Don't let diet and clothes and dialect and different forms of worship distract you from the essence of the Supreme One, which is pure love and Oneness.

Now let me talk about the meditation that has been mentioned extensively. This is the way I have been taught through my prayers and vision. It is similar to the way *Bapuji* has spoken about but there is a little variation.

Sit down comfortably, preferably with a straight back. You can sit on a chair resting the back with a cushion or tie yourself in a knot in any yoga posture. For a while just observe your breath. Eyes shut, observe your breath during inhalation and exhalation. Simple breathing but try to make your exhalation longer than your inhalation. The ideal ratio is for every second of inhalation, have as many seconds of exhalation as possible but don't force it. It should come naturally. Yogis for every second of inhalation can extend their exhalation to thirty two seconds and even longer, but then yogis don't have any other work to do so they can go about life doing all these funny things. You just try to make sure that your exhalation is effortlessly longer than your inhalation. Don't try to do anything unnatural.

Sit in front of the rising Sun if possible, if not, in front of a candle or flame or then even in front of a lit bulb. Imagine the light coming from the source, be it the Sun, candle, flame or bulb, filling your body up. Lighting your body within and imagine your body filled within with golden light. Start with imagining it and with little practice you will see your body filled with light. Give the affirmation that "I am the Golden Light as I come from the Great Golden Flame. I am not the body. I am the Spirit. I come from the Divine Source". For a few days, as and when you have time, just do this simple meditation. Once you are cool about this, after filling yourself up with the Golden Light, imagine this Light, moving upwards. The Golden Light within you, moves upwards from the top of your head and let it keep moving upwards to the Source of Light; the Great Flame; the Source of all Existence. Thus the Light is within your body, it is also travelling to the Great Flame, and now the Light connects you to the Great Flame. It is like a beam, and now the beam joins you and the Great Flame, making both of you one entity, and then you are enveloped with the Golden Light. You are in your body. You are also in the Great Flame. Give whatever affirmation you so desire. From the Great Flame, see your affirmation spread to all of creation. Ask for peace and wellbeing in all of creation. Ask for love and laughter for yourself, your loved ones and for all of creation. Ask for health and prosperity for yourself, loved ones, and all of creation. Imagine the Golden Light from the Great Flame enter you through the top of your head, fill you up, and through you spread to all of creation. Ask for peace for all those in the physical plane, those in the spirit plane and those in between. Pray for the Light to reach every corner of creation but also every corner of all spirit dimensions, thus helping all to move towards the Light. To move away from darkness into the Light, moving and merging with the Great Flame. Know that you are one with the Great Flame and the Great Flame is one with you.

Now imagine the Golden Light, slowly healing every part of you. The healing energy enters you from the top of your head and slowly travel within you, from the skull, into your eyes, nose, mouth, throat, neck, slowly moving downwards, cleansing, energizing and harmonizing, every part of your being. Let the Golden Light reach the soles of your feet, and move into the Earth. Now the Great Flame, You and Mother Earth are one. Now feel the pure love and selflessness of Mother Earth's energy fill you up and envelope you. In return you become the medium to pass on to Mother Earth the Golden Light from the Golden Flame through you. She needs all the love and energy. She has only given. It is right that you give Her through you the Golden Light too. See the Oneness through Her. She is all giving. Mother Earth only gives. She never asks in return. No matter how much we plunder Her, She only gives us. So become one with Her and through Her you will become one with all living beings on our planet. Give affirmations of love and that nobody should go hungry, or thirsty, or without shelter and medicine. That let peace prevail. Let there be only peace and harmony. Every time we eat or drink, let nobody go hungry or thirsty. Let there be peace, joy and laughter. Through the Golden Flame and through Mother Earth, you will become one with all of creation. And the Golden Flame, Mother Earth, and you become One. Once you feel you have done this, slowly return to yourself, first from Mother Earth and then from the Great Flame. Rub your palms and caress your eyes and face and then open your eyes.

Then if you want light up a cigarette, read the newspaper, curse the politicians and go about life.

18

The fact of the matter is no matter what you think or do. No matter who you believe in or don't. Whether you believe in the philosophy of the 108 or the stages of heaven and hell or the explanation of creation, it doesn't really matter. What is most important is that you believe that you are loved and your Master is with you, along with the army of *Light Workers* and that you are never alone.

No matter what the world thinks of you. No matter if you are successful or not in the eyes of the world. No matter, no matter, no matter what, the only reality lies within you. It is within each one of us. It always has been. It always will be. Heaven and hell; happiness and sorrow; humility and pride; love and lust; sanity and madness; silence and chaos; joy and depression; all that should be and all that which isn't; it's all within us.

Forget philosophies and bugger ideologies professed by one and all. Find your own path. As long as you want to make your Master happy and proud of you, you can't go wrong. Yes we will mess up on a daily basis. That's ok. Don't get complacent about it but don't flog yourself too. Life and one's Karma anyway do a darn good job in the department of flogging one and all. Just don't let go of the need and urge to walk the path. Sometimes due to past lifetimes and experiences of this, the path will be more difficult or at least seem more frustrating for you than the rest. It's ok. Believe in the fact that if you have truly surrendered to the Light and eventually all darkness will fade away, as you move towards the Light, a day not far from now, you will become Light yourself. It is when moving towards the Sun that one feels maximum heat. Once you are in the Sun, you become the Sun too and thus become Light yourself. The Sun doesn't feel its own heat. So don't get scared of the heat.

Don't let petty people distract you. Don't let your own chaos in the head, dim the sound of silence. Keep walking. When you fall, get up, dust yourself of all the muck and sludge, and keep walking the path. None of us is perfect. We all have our personal demons and our Cross to bear. It's fine. Only you and your Master know your reality. Life may not seem fair and God may seem not to hear your plea. Neither of this is true. Life is fair and God is within, listening to every word you speak with your heart and most importantly, hoping you begin to listen to what the Voice wants you to hear.

Life is about exhaling. Not about holding one's breath.

Whichever faith and religion you belong to or don't want to belong to; it matters little, as long as you believe that God has no personal vendetta against you. He doesn't. He can't. If we are the Spirit in the body, then that Spirit has come through the Creator and the Spirit is the Creator. If nothing can be created or destroyed in the cosmos and it only changes form, so believe, you and I have just changed forms, but our essence truly comes from the Source and thus we too are the Source.

Believe that soft voice within you, when you are calm. Hear the sigh of the soul, when you slowly connect with your breath. That's the soul song. And the music is that of Oneness. Our only priority is to spread whatever happiness and joy we possibly can. Help others when we can. Make the Old Man grin once in a while. He must be tired. Seeing the mess we have created of our individual universe; which is oneself. Forget the *Brähmāñḍs* all over creation. Focus on your *Brähmāñḍ*, which is your being.

They say we come with nothing and go back with nothing. That's a load of undiluted horse shit; the greatest lie. We come with our Karmas and go back with our Karmas. That's the truth and that's the greatest reality. And the ramification of Karma is beyond all religions, all ideologies, all philosophies and is one's real reflection of who we truly are and the only person who is with you through this dance of life, is one's Master; whether be it your higher self or your Guru; the one person who truly loves you, and who loves selflessly and patiently. To live to make the Master happy and proud of one self, is according to me, the only priority worth having and trying to live up to.

Call on one's Master, the Archangels, Angels, the Oneness Family and know for sure They will be by your side. Call on Them as a child would to one's parents and elders. They will stand by you and if you are calm you will hear the sigh of Heaven.

May the Oneness walk with you, paving your path with Light, a song in your heart, joy in your eyes and wellbeing in your soul.

Be blessed always.

Jai Baba. Jai Maa.

•••

Glossary

A

Ādam ko Khudā mat kaho; Ādam Khudā nahin; magar Khudā ke noor se Ādam judā nahin - Don't call Adam God; Adam is not God; But from the Light of God, Adam is not separate

Agatya Vāṇis - The Subtle Voice of the Cosmos

Ahañkār - Ego

Akāl Mooṛt -The changeless form

Akāl Puṛakh - Being timeless and deathless

Akāl Puṛakh, Akāl Takht; Akāl Mooṛt - That which *Kāl* or time and death cannot eat up

Ākāri Ātmās - Spirit-forms

Akartā - A non-doer

Ākāś se Pareh - Beyond the Skies

Amar Avināśi - Forever and immortal, indestructible

Amar Lok – A place where there is no limit of age and limitation of birth and death

Amar Lok - Immortal World

Amar Tatva - The Eternal Infinite Elements

Amrut - Nectar of Immortality

Ānand, Nijānand Swarūpam - Pure Supreme Bliss, Image of the One in Self Delight or the Divine Joyful Image of the Own Self

Anant Koti - Innumerable crores

Anjanā or Ājñā Chakra - The Third Eye *Chakra*

Aṇu – Atom, a speck

Anulom-Vilom - *Prāṇāyam*

Arabo and Kharabo - Trillions and hundreds-of-billion

Ārti - Lighting oil lamps as a prayer ritual

Ashta - Eight

Asur Ātmās - Animal souls

Atal Lok - Pig-headed or Rigid Land

Ātmā - The Individual Soul

ĀtmàSwarūp Nu Jñān - Knowledge of the soul-form

Aum Tat Sat - I Am That

Avatār - One who is *Nyārā* from *Janam and Maran*

Avatārit - To Appear or simply Emerge

Avyakt Duniya - Ethereal World

B

Bayhuđ na Paṛam Pitā - The Founding Father of the Infinite

Bayhuđ Nu Paṛam Dhām - The Supreme Abode of the Infinite

Bēj Rūp Avasthā - The State of Sprouting or the Burgeoning stage

Betā -Son

Bhagwan - God

Bhāgya - Destiny

Bhāvnā - Intent

Bhu – Earth

Brāhṁā - Creator

Brāhṁācharya - Celibacy

Brāhṁāñḍs – Galaxies

Buđhi – Intellect, wisdom

Buđhi-Siđhi - Power of Wisdom and Manifestation of Knowledge

C

Chaitañya Swarūp - The All Powerful Divine Image

Chandra Dev – God of the Moon

Chapals - Slippers

D

Dasam Dwār - The tenth door or 10th *Chakra*

Devatās - Demi Gods

Dhàṛma Guru - The Teacher

Dhàṛti, Jal, Agni, Vāyu, and *Ākāś* - Earth, Water, Fire, Wind and Ether

Divya - Divine

Divya Ātmās - Divine Souls

Divya Druśti - Divine Vision

Divya Swarūp Nu Jñān - Knowledge of the Divine Self

G

Gati - Speed

Gītā - The Hindu Holy text that is a part of the Māhābhāṛāta

Grahast Āśrăm - Living the life of a householder

Grām Dev or *Devi* - Village God or Goddess

Gūṇa - Attributes and characteristics

Guṇās - Qualities

Gurudwaras – Place of worship for those following the Sikh religion

H

Hisāb-kitāb - Accounts

Huđ - Limit

I

Indṛiyās - The five astral sense organs

Ishta Dev - One's Primordial God, Goddess or Guru

J

Jaisā ann, vaisā mun - What one eats one thinks and feels

Jal Samādhi - Water Liberation

Jānvar Buđhi -One with the mentality of an animal

Jēvan Mukti - Body made of *Amrut Taŧva* or the Eternal Element while alive

Jñān - Knowledge

Jñān dān – Charity of knowledge, spreading knowledge, educating people, sponsoring education

Jñān Jal – Waters of Wisdom

Jñān Sāgar - Oceans of knowledge

Jñān Sñān – A bath of knowledge

Jyotir Brāhṁ - *Paṛam Māhā Brāhṁā*, Bright Light

K

Kāl – Death, time

Kāl Chakra – The wheel of time

Kāl ke panje se chudao; hey Mā Ashta Bhavani – Please release me from the clutches of *Kāl*, O Mother *Ashta Bhavāni*

Kaḷā - Celestial degree of the soul, spiritual power

Kalp Vruksh – Wish-fulfilling tree of manifestations

Kānchān Kāyā - Crystal-clear body

Kāṛaṇ Śarēr - Causal body

Kāṛaṇsaṛi - Reason of being

Karma *Bandhan* - Bondage of destined Karma, Karmic entanglement

Karmayogi - Involved in meditative action

Kṛodh - Anger

L

Loukik – Tangible, substantial, corporal, material world

M

Māhā Asurs - Negative souls

Māhā dān - Greatest of all charities

Māhā Taŧva - Divine Light

Māhā Vakyās - Phrases and sentences containing profound wisdom

Mālik – Master

Manañ and *Chintan* - Deep meditation and contemplation

Manomay Sharēr - The body of the mind and heart

Manomayē Vikās - Spiritual cleansing and progress

Manuśya Lok -The human world

Māyā - Illusion of identifying with the body and the five senses

Māyāvi - Aliens

Moh - Desire

Mokśa - Liberation

Mrutyu Kāl -The Clutches of Death and Karma

Mrutyu Lok - The World of Death

Mukti - The merger of the soul into the One from which it has originated

Mun – Heart

N

Năkśăţṛăs - Planetary configurations

Naṣhto mohā, samruti labhḍā, ichchā mātra vidyā- That person will have no wish, want; will be a *Vairāgi,* disenchanted and unattached

Natak – Drama

Nih-Sañkalp –Without thoughts, intents

Nirākār - Formless

Niśchay - A confirmation or a firm decision

Nishkām -Selfless

Nyārā from *Janam and Maran* – Beyond birth and death

P

Paṛam – Supreme, pure

Paṛam Ānañd Swaṛūpam - The Prime Form of Bliss and Liberating Peace

Paṛam Ātmā - Godhood or the Supreme Soul

Paṛam Ātmā - The Cosmic Soul or Creator

Paṛam Ātmà Swarūp - The Divine Supreme Soul Image of One's Self, his or her own *Paṛam* or Supreme Image

Paṛam Ātmās - The Supreme Souls

Paṛam Pitā - The Founding or Supreme Father of the Infinite

Paṛam Pṛakāś - Supreme Divine Radiance, *Paṛam* Light

Paṛam Pṛakāś - Supreme Eternal Light

Paṛam Rachnā - Supreme Creation

Paṛam Satya - Of the highest supreme truth

Paṛam Tatva - Supreme Element

Pavitra Ātmāṣ - Pure souls

Pitru Lok - The Abode of Ancestors

Pitru Tarpan Karna- Giving solace to the souls of our ancestors through an offering of food or *Bhog*

Pṛakāś Swarūp – Enlightened version

Pṛakāśmai - Enlightened

Prakruti - Woman energy

Prāṇa - Divine energy

Prāṇāyam - Yogic breathing

Prêt Ātmās - Earthbound souls, ghosts

Prithvi Samādhi - Surrendering to mother earth for liberation

Purusharth - Appropriate action

R

Rachanas - Creations

Rāgās - Ancient Indian musical compositions

Rāg-Dwesh - Anger and Rage

Rākśasa -Demon

Rāśis - Zodiac Signs

Rath - Chariot

Rooh - Soul

Rūp - Image

Rūśimuni, Tapasvi – Sage

S

Sadhana - Devotion

Sāgar Manthan – Mythological event of churning the ocean

Sākāri - The physical-forms

Śakti - Energy

Śaktis - Energies, power

Samadhi - Liberation

Samadhi Avastha - State of Liberation

Saṁpūrṇa - Complete within itself

Sampūrna Nirvikāri - Sinless and pure

Sañchālan - Management

Sañkalp - A promise, an oath, a vow, a thought, a word, a decision, a dedicated pledge and a determination

Sanskār - Value system and conditioning

Sañskārs - One's nature and conditioning or soul journey

Śāñti - Peace

Śāñtrūp - Image of Silence

Sanyāsa Āśrăm – A phase when one goes in search of God leaving the family and responsibility of a householder living the life of an ascetic

Sapt Ruśis - Seven sages

Śāstṛās - Holy Indian texts like *Upanishads, Vedas, Puṙāṇas*

Ṣāṣwat - Necessarily permanent and that which lasts forever

Satya Pradhān Ātmās - Truth manifesting or truth dominating souls

Saŧva, Rajas and *Tamas* - Three basic natural dispositions or characteristics

Shraḍha Itni Honi Chahiye Ke Guru Ko Hila Dey - One's faith in one's Guru should be so strong and pure that it shakes the very Guru

Šiva - Destroyer

Somras –Astral liquor

Sṛuśti - Nature

Sṛuśti Chakra - The complete creation of the world or nature

Sthool - The gross or the physical world

Sufi Darghas – Place of worship

Sukh and *Ṣanti* - Peace and joy

Śukra - Mercury

Sūkśṃ - Subtle body

Sūkśṃ Vatan -The Astral Worlds

Svabhāv - Character

Swāhā - Obliterate

T

Tadapti Hai - Suffers

Takht - The throne of the timeless and deathless One

Tapasyā - Spiritual penance and austerity

Tapasyās - Spiritual exercises, penance

Tatva - Element

Total *Prälai* - Complete destruction on earth

U

Upvās -Upar Vās Karna Hai

V

Vairāgya - Detachment

Vairāgya - Disenchantment from worldly matters

Vāyu - Thoughts

Vāyu Mandàḷ -Atmosphere

Vidhi - Procedure

Vikār - Decay

Vināś-heen -That which cannot be destroyed and is essentially eternal

Virāt Rūp - The Majestic Form

Viśnu - Sustainer

Viśwa Kalyānkāri - Proactive in world welfare or progress

Viśwa Parivartak – Individual helpful in changing the world

Viśwa Parivàṛtăn - Transformation of the world

Viśwa Seva Dhāri - Service oriented

Vrutis - Disposition or characteristic

Vyakt Duniya - Physical World

Y

Yagyā - Holy fire for offerings as per Hindu tradition

Yog - Meditative state

Yog Agni - Fire of meditation

Yog-Śakti - Through the power of the meditative state

Yojan - An old metric system of measuring distance

Yonis - Wombs

Vishwa Parivartak Iswariya Vidhyalaya

Vishwa Parivartak Iswariya Vidhyalaya was founded in 1997 by *Dashrathbhai Patel*, who is lovingly referred to as *Bapuji*.

In 1997 *Bapuji* laid the foundation of the Ashram in *Ahmedabad, Gujarat* with aid from a few blessed souls with the holy intention of spreading Oneness and Knowledge about the transformation of the cosmos towards positive energy heralding the Golden Age of Righteousness. He has attempted to present to the world the Divine Knowledge which should be understood, realized and put to use for the benediction of the world.

<u>THE WEST ZONE</u>

Vishwa Parivartak Iswariya Vidhyalaya,
At Chenpur, Near New Ranip, Ahmedabad, Gujarat.
India

<u>THE NORTH ZONE</u>

Vishwa Parivartak Iswariya Vidhyalaya,
At Village Aklimpur, Badshapur - Tikli Road,
Gurgaon – Haryana. India

<u>ALTERNATIVETY CALL /EMAIL</u>

Neeru Tandon: + 91 93509 39342 /
info@discoveryofnewworld.com

Anant Patel: + 91 92277 57852 / anant98251@yahoo.com

Sakshi Patel: +91 97141 37575 / saakshi1985@gmail.com

OFFICIAL WEBSITE

www.discoveryofnewworld.com

SOCIAL MEDIA ADDRESSES

YOUTUBE: youtube.com/anant98251

FACEBOOK US: discoveryofnewworld.com

Author of ten published books and a documentary film maker, Ruzbeh N Bharucha began his writing career in his final year of college, by editing and publishing a magazine called *Venture.*

In 1992, he was appointed Associate Editor for *Special Audience Publication*, and two years later become the Chief of a first weekly newspaper in Pune, *The Pune Tribune*, published in English and Marathi by A. K. Bhalla.

Ruzbeh N Bharucha

In 1995, he was appointed the Executive Editor, Business Publication Division, *The Indian Express.* In 2000, he edited magazines on the paranormal, mysticism, new age, and travel, for S. B. Associates.

His articles have been featured in various publications, namely, *The Times of India, Free Press, The Indian Express, Maharashtra Herald, Sunday Observer, Jam-e-Jamshed and The Afternoon.*

In 2000, his first book, *The Last Marathon,* a journey into the world of the paranormal was published by *Sainathann Communication.* The book in its third edition now been published by Full Circle Publishing.

In 2002, the book *Devi's Emerald,* a book on the abundant grace and compassion on *Ma Mookambika Devi* and her medium *Swamiji* was published by *Vakil, Simon* and *Faffer.* It was reprinted in 2004 published by Shree Mookambika Bhakta Mandali.

Both books deal with the paranormal and spiritual forces in the Cosmos.

In 2004, Fusion Publishers published his book, *Shadows In Cages.* A soul stirring book that is the first of its kind which deals with mothers and their children living in Indian prisons throwing light on the various emotional aspects of what women inmates feel and share with their children. The book is in its second edition and has also been translated in *Hindi* and *Marathi.*

The book, *Shadows In Cages,* was published and released for the International market by the Himalayan Institute Press, Pennsylvania, USA.

The Author scripted and directed a documentary called *I Believe I Can Fly.* The documentary gives a glimpse of the life of mothers and their children in Indian prisons. The twenty minute documentary has been screened in *Singapore, Sri Lanka, India* and in the *US.*

In 2005, Fusion Publishers released his first work of fiction, *Rest In Pieces.* The book is peppered with humour and hilarious situations but the undercurrent of sadness is as real as the morning's screaming news deadlines. A hilarious yet heart-wrenching story.

His documentary, *Yamuna Gently Weeps,* a film on the demolition of one of the biggest slums in the world, the Yamuna Pushta, has been screened at various *International Human Rights Film Festivals* and *Universities* world wide.

Yamuna Gently Weeps, also a three hundred-page book with heart-wrenching photographs and interviews with slum dwellers, politicians, renowned town planners, environmentalists and activists, was released in August 2006.

His book, *The Fakir,* launched in October 2007, is already in its seventh edition and was on the top of the best seller list in December 2007. *The Fakir* has been translated in *Hindi, Marathi* and *German,* and is also soon to be released in *Punjabi, Bengali, Gujarati, Tamil* and *Bulgarian.*

In early 2008 the first book on the emotional and mental trauma of juvenile delinquents in India, *My God Is A Juvenile*

Delinquent, was published. The book has been included in the reading list of all judicial academies by a central order.

His documentary on AIDS and HIV in the Tihar Prison, *Sehat...Wings Of Freedom,* sponsored by the United Nations, was selected and screened for *The XVII International AIDS Conference,* in Mexico, in August 2008.

From 2008 to 2011 the author was Executive Editor, of the 4th D Wellbeing Journal, a widely read national magazine on physical, emotional and spiritual wellbeing, with a print run of over 60,000 copies per month.

In 2009, his publishing house, Sainathann Publications, released two books, one on *Shri Ram Thakur* and a Bengali book on *Sai Baba of Shirdi.*

In 2010, *The Fakir* was soon followed by an equally successful sequel, *The Fakir...The Journey Continues* which was launched at the end of 2010 by Full Circle Publications. The book was published in German in 2011. The book is soon to be released in its *Hindi* and *Punjabi* editions.

Both the books have been re-printed several times and are now considered to be among the best books on spiritual and paranormal literature.

The Fakir: Thoughts and Prayers was published in 2011, a collection of profoundly transformative and powerful messages and prayers from *The Fakir* books that have touched the lives of many all over the world.

The author's documentary films, *Yamuna Gently Weeps, I Believe I Can Fly and SEHAT...Wings Of Freedom* were screened at the ASIAN FILM FESTIVAL PUNE in December 2011.

Bringing in light into the lives of those who are visually impaired... *The Fakir* has also been printed in its Braille version that has been distributed to all centres all over India in 2012.

In 2013, *The Aum Of All Things,* was published, a non-fiction book on life, death, the world of spirits, Oneness and manipulation of the five elements to transform one's life.

Other works by the author

BOOKS:

The Last Marathon
A journey into the world of the paranormal

Devi's Emerald
A book on MAA MOOKAMBIKA DEVI and HER Medium Swamiji

The Fakir
The one who makes the thunder roar also hears the butterfly sigh

The Fakir... The journey continues
The reality of life is that it never ends...

The Fakir... Thoughts and Prayers

Shadows in Cages
Mother and Child in Indian Prisons

Yamuna Gently Weeps
A journey into the demolition of one of the biggest slums in the world, Yamuna Pushta

My God is a Juvenile Delinquent
The first English book on the emotional and mental trauma of juvenile delinquents in India

Rest in Pieces

DOCUMENTARIES:

I Believe I can fly
Mother and child in Indian Prisons

Yamuna Gently Weeps
A journey into the Yamuna Pushta Slum Demolition

SEHAT... Wings of Freedom
HIV and AIDS awareness Programme in Tihar Prison

Other titles by Ruzbeh N. Bhaurcha

The Fakir

The One who makes the thunder roar, also hears a butterfly sigh.

A hippie with an inclination for suicide, a fakir with a quaint sense of humour, a journey that might change your life forever...

The Fakir, is a breathtaking spiritual odyssey to your inner self, where God and Master dwell. Experience the joy of being alive, learn the simple yet life altering philosophy of compassion towards all, and heal yourself by taking that first step towards CHANGE.

A fascinating story that explores complex issues in a simple, very easy-to-understand, accessible way — karma, divine action, life after death, spirit communication, the power of prayer, faith and forgiveness, energy and healing; the search for God in goodness and most importantly being constantly attuned with your Master.

The Fakir, shows you not only how to live... but also how to die.

Other titles by Ruzbeh N. Bhaurcha

The Fakir

The Journey Continues...

The reality of life is
that it never ends...

Rudra who always wanted to die but found it hard to exist... finally passes over.

The all knowing FAKIR who guides him every step of the way and Rudra embark on a journey to the higher realms of the spirit world... and experience its all encompassing magic... the magnificent power of unconditional love, wisdom and surrender.

A gripping story told with humour, it weaves in and out of the physical and astral realms where the seeker transforms into the lover, and begins to understand the ancient law of free will, the extraordinary power of human thought, choices and intent that shape our lives in both the worlds.

THE FAKIR reveals how complete love for the MASTER is like a mighty river of light... navigating us constantly through the turbulent waters of karma... addictions... ignorance and merging the seeker into the ocean of pure consciousness.

Death is a myth. Life never ends. Ignorance does.